Midlife MEDITATIONS

FOR

WOMEN

MAUREEN BRADY

HarperSanFrancisco

A Division of HarperCollins*Publishers*

Grateful acknowledgment is made for permission to reprint the following:

An excerpt from an art exhibit by Sybil Adelman Sage in Bad Girls I, The New Museum of Contemporary Art, New York, 1993, "Why doesn't a 60 year old woman. . . ." Reprinted with permission of the author.

The following passages from *Lesbians at Midlife: The Creative Transition*, edited by B. Sang, J. Warshow, and A. Smith, San Francisco, California, 1991, are reprinted with permission of Spinsters Ink, P.O. Box 300170, Minneapolis, Minnesota 55403; "In the early . . . a grand purpose." Jacqueline H. Gentry and Fay M. Seifert, page 277; "It really isn't . . . what am I?" Jewelle Gomez, page 77; "Living in the white world . . . and there's beauty in that." Muriel Miguel, page 205; "I allow myself . . . erotic ally." Joan Nestle, page 182; "I have come to believe . . . and I've become more whole." Matile Rothschild, page 98; "So, yes, now I . . . to be 'normal.'" Susan Turner, page 63.

FIRST EDITION

Library of Congress Cataloging-in-Publication Data
Brady, Maureen.
Midlife : Meditations for women / Maureen Brady.
p. cm.
Includes index.
ISBN 0–06–251148–3 (pbk. : acid-free paper)
1. Middle aged women—Prayer-books and devotions—English. 2. Middle aged persons—Prayer-books and devotions—English. 3. Menopause—Religious aspects—Meditations. 4. Midlife crisis—Religious aspects—Meditations.
5. Twelve-step programs—Religious aspects—Meditations. 6. Devotional calendars. I. Title.
BL624.5.B73 1995
291.4'3—dc20   94-24328

94 95 96 97 98 ❖ HAD 10 9 8 7 6 5 4 3 2 1

This edition is printed on acid-free paper that meets the American National Standards Institute Z39.48 Standard.

ACKNOWLEDGMENTS

I would like to gratefully acknowledge all of the women I have quoted from in these meditations for their many thoughts, with which they have inspired me.

I also acknowledge my editors, Barbara Moulton and Lisa Bach, for their careful work with this book.

No woman or man escapes undergoing a midlife transition except by dying young. Yet we live in a culture in which there are no rituals for this passage. In ancient myths and in some other cultures, the changes of midlife are seen as involving more than just the body. The psyche longs for a deepening of the spiritual and emotional realms. What may have once been very satisfying to a person in more youthful years—career ambition, the desire to excel in a sport, the wish to form and raise a family, pride in sexual appeal and prowess—ceases to satisfy. In our youth-glorifying society, we feel desperate when we begin to lose satisfaction with youthful desires. Though we may feel tired, we try harder. Surely if we race faster and harder, we think, we will feel those satisfactions again. And yet we only frustrate ourselves, until finally we discover that the old satisfactions are no longer what we need.

In many myths about maturation, one goes to the top of a mountain and surveys the larger picture of the world below. One grows quiet, receptive, even reverent, and open to the guidance of a higher spirit within or perhaps of the spirit of Nature. When one returns to the everyday world, it is with a new perspective. From middle age, as from the top of a mountain, it is possible to see both ways—backward to birth and forward to death. One sees that the limit of one's own death makes it time to awaken more clearly to one's purpose. With this perspective, it is possible to relax or even give up pursuing the satisfactions of old desires and to settle peacefully into new ways of seeking meaning and contentment in alignment with one's age and nature.

For women, menopause is the opportune time to attend to and mark this passage. Yet because it has been overlooked and even hidden in our culture, menopause has become an experience cloaked in dread rather than one anticipated for its riches. Now that we are beginning to talk more openly about menopause, why not use it as the perfect container for our midlife transition? Why not enter it thoughtfully and with a spirit of adventure, anticipating our hot flashes as alchemy—the fire that will energize our changes? Is there anything more succulent than a fruit fully ripened? But to fully ripen we must be willing to be awake and aware. Let us not deny or miss our ripening because we are focused backward, trying to look, act, or be some other, more youthful age. A Buddhist *gatha* I hang on my wall to remind me to live in the present says:

Let me respectfully remind you—
Life and death are of supreme importance
Time swiftly passes by, and opportunity is lost
Each of us should strive to awaken
. . . . awaken
Take heed. Do not squander your life.

Midlife was written to help you make your midlife journey one of deepening acceptance and discovery of all that is ripening in you. These meditations offer positive reflections on the changes you are going through or have already gone through. They can be read daily or by subject by using the index. May they help you embrace each day as it is given and discover the grace of receiving each gift the day offers. And may you be inspired, as I was, by all the women whose wisdom I have quoted here.

Renewal

New Year's Day is an event at the dump. Everyone wants a fresh start. Menopause is an event, too. A gradual sifting and sorting to see who we are as our wombs cease shedding.

MARIANNE

At the beginning of each year, we are prone to taking inventories. We do little rituals to clean out some of the clutter from the past; we visualize what we desire for the coming year. We are reminded that time is passing—that, as mortals, our years on earth are limited.

For those of us who've reached midlife, the year's beginning is an especially useful reminder because we want to awaken more fully with each passing year. We want to check our direction and make sure we are on course. If we have veered away from seeking and serving our highest purposes, we want to reorient ourselves. We are valuable. Our lives are of great consequence. Each year is an opportunity to be faithful and loving to our being.

I renew my commitment to attend to myself lovingly this day and this year.

Transformation

> By means of an image we are often able to hold on to our lost belongings.
>
> **COLETTE**

What image can anchor us as we go through menopause? Many of us feel as though we are losing our belongings. We may have emotional upheavals—depression, flashes of rage, crying jags—for which we can't identify any cause. We may be saddened that the months are no longer marked by the predictable rhythm of a period. We knew our bodies then better than we do now. We knew when our emotions were being seasoned with PMS. We knew the sense of calm that occurred once menstruation took place.

We need images of transformation. The end of the old year begets the new year. The end of our childbearing years begets our self-bearing years. We are birthing women of wisdom. At the end of this tunnel of turmoil, let us see the image of a stalwart Crone, a woman not over the hill but on the top of the mountain, seeing birth from one perspective, death from another.

I hold in my mind's eye images to sustain me as I go through my Change.

Influence

The influence you exert is through your own life and what you become yourself.

ELEANOR ROOSEVELT

By midlife we begin to understand life's interrelations—how we each truly do influence one another. We affect our loved ones by how we think of them and treat them. We affect those our work reaches. We affect our community—from the smaller community of our immediate world to the larger community of the earth—by the attitudes we carry and the spirit we bring to all we do.

If we are experiencing a midlife crisis, we might stop to take an honest look at who we have become. Did we mean to be more influential? Have we failed to take ourselves seriously? Are we acting as though we are invisible, as though we don't matter? However we feel we may be lacking, now is the time to understand and use ourselves to our best ability. Now is the time to awaken those aspects of ourselves we have left dormant. Now is the time to recognize that we are citizens of the world and can act upon the world in the ways we desire.

Today, I recognize and respect how I influence myself and others.

Croning

Shall we shamelessly affirm one of the unique aspects of womanhood by developing ways to celebrate menopause? Although psychologists recognize that both men and women undergo a major change in midlife, only with the rise of the second wave of feminism in the last twenty years have many women begun to see this transition as an opportune time for declaring oneself a Wise Woman.

Why not gather our friends around us, hold a ritual celebration, and see ourselves as being born anew into the latter half of our century? Let us also take this opportunity to reflect on our lives to see which fields we would like to make more fertile.

I am free to declare myself a Wise Woman—one whose power is within me as I grow into older ages.

Creativity

When we are living as our unique selves, we find we have a rich creativity available to us. . . . We love into existence that which we wish to create. I believe that what we create also contains the love that brought us into existence.

RUTH SCHWEITZER-MORDECAI

Midlife is when many of us blossom fully into our creativity. This blossoming may mean developing further a form of creative expression; it may mean greater receptivity, opening our inner doors to learn from the creations of others. It may mean both.

Creative expression often arises from the urge to demonstrate wholeness, not perfection. Our soul seeks more breathing room. We continually desire that human nature be represented in the forms we understand. This verifies our existence and aligns us with our creator, whatever we envision that force to be.

Today, I freely allow creative energy to flow through me.

Risk

> Actually I have a lot in common with the cow that Jumped over the moon. Did she know where she was going? I'm sure she didn't, exactly, but she knew she had to do it.
>
> **MARY DALY**

We often wish we could see the outcome of a change before we begin it. Knowing the outcome, we could bypass our doubting questions, such as, Do I *really* want to do this? Sometimes we run around the same track for months or years because we are afraid of taking a risk.

Menopause comes upon us regardless of our desire to control time. It reminds us that there are many events over which we have no control. We enter menopause because our body tells us we have arrived at this life transition. In light of our changing physical landscape, this is an expedient time to jump over the moon in other ways. Since we are already coming apart—and rearranging to come together again—why not reawaken those visions we long neglected because they required taking a risk?

How did the cow know she had to jump? How do we know? We do know, don't we?

I venture forth toward change, despite my fears of risking the security of stasis.

Perimenopause

Now my monthly bleeding is precious. . . . This companion of more than thirty years is preparing to leave; I feel her restless stirrings, the way her attention wanders, how irregular she's become. I know my life will be different when she's gone.

GRANDMOTHER
GROWTH
(SUSUN S. WEED)

We may have dreaded our menses in earlier years and even joked that we would be glad when they ended. Yet when we reach the age when they become irregular, summoning our attention to the fact they will soon be gone, we find ourselves saddened and regretful. We remember how these periods began when we were girls—how they meant we were becoming women.

Whether or not we have had children, we all experience grief at knowing that the potential of our fertility is coming to a close.

Our lives will be different without our monthly bleeding. There is no denying an imminent change in our lives. But if we consciously choose to awaken to the meanings of this change, we can understand it as the point to be satisfied with our youth and to look ahead, to use our wisdom to make our older years full and inspiring.

*Rather than disregard the signs of coming change,
I choose to wake up and be aware of them.*

Becoming Ourselves

As life goes on it becomes tiring to keep up the character you invented for yourself, and so you relapse into individuality and become more like yourself every day. This is sometimes disconcerting for those around you, but a great relief to the person concerned.

AGATHA CHRISTIE

Who else would we become but ourselves? And what a relief it is! When we invent a false front, we have to devote ourselves to holding it together, evaluating its effectiveness, revising it— essentially performing. We live with the dissonance of expressing feelings contradictory to those we have within us. Remember the discomfort of deliberately holding a smile through a wedding or a party, despite the real feelings we had beneath the surface?

It is exhilarating to realize that we are being ourselves— no performing—and that we are enough. By midlife, understanding that our time is limited helps us know that we do not want to squander our energy. We want our actions and feelings to arise straight from our cores. We want to follow our instincts. We learn that we only needed to love much of what we once thought we needed to change about ourselves.

I am growing into myself.

Mystery

I got the general impression [as a child looking at wall maps] that Canada was the same size as the world, which somehow or other fitted into it, or the other way around, and that in the world and Canada the sun was always shining and everything was dry and glittering. At the same time, I knew perfectly well that this was not true.

ELIZABETH BISHOP

When we are children, the range of our imagination is unparalleled. We do not try to think something through, from point A to point B, in a linear and rational fashion. Remembering this now may bring us closer to our spirit.

As we grow up, we learn necessary restraint, which spills over into unnecessary restraint. We acquire the illusion that we must make sense of everything and that what we can't make sense of must not be real. We cease to attend to those aspects of life that cannot be explained. Our spiritual dimensions, disregarded, drop off to sleep.

Our Change presents an appropriate time to let our spiritual dimension reawaken, to realize that mystery is a crucial part of a vivid life. We do not need to understand everything; in fact, much of life's experience is beyond us.

Today, I embrace the mysterious way life unfolds before me.

Postmenopausal Zest

For every grieving Demeter suffering from empty-nest depression, there seems to be—as anthropologist Margaret Mead remarked—another woman with a surge of P.M.Z., "post-menopausal zest."

JEAN SHINODA BOLEN, M.D.

We hear too little about postmeno-pausal zest. Who are these women? Where does this energy come from? Jean Shinoda Bolen, who writes about how the energies of the goddesses exist in every woman, visualizes this energy as a new Goddess shining through.

Many women say they feel that they've come into a new wave of energy when menopause ends. The turbulent mood swings level out, and we get a sense of well-being, of floating on a placid ocean. Our hormones have established a new balance, our confidence rises, and we are ready to meet life head-on. We direct ourselves toward our own goals more freely, with less concern for the goals of others. We enjoy our own company. We discover in ourselves new talents and desires and take pleasure in expressing them.

I let out the woman of postmenopausal zest in me.

Individuation

Separation from the collective affect and its contagious effect is an aspect of individuation.

MARIE-LOUISE VON FRANZ

Remember the contagious effect of the collective affect in adolescence? If we cannot remember our own adolescence well, we can surely see this in our children or in the teenagers we know.

Posturing is of prime importance, as we try to emulate the *coolest* person we know. This posturing was most evident when we began to differentiate ourselves from our family and its collective affect.

Many years later, we realize that our rebellion did not accomplish individuation; it only gave us an alternate set of collective values. One of the challenges of midlife is to seek a more individual expression of the Self. We are aided in this by the security of our age and experience. After all, we have learned that whenever we deviate from the collective opinion or feeling, regardless of any discomfort we might encounter, we survive.

I relax into an individual expression of myself and appreciate the spaciousness that comes of manifesting who I am.

Hot Flashes

When my hot flashes come, I think of them as power surges. I think that they are heating me up for some great change.

JANE

When we resist the expression of any energy, it only enlarges the sensation of the energy. When we surrender to it and move with it, we experience harmony.

We do not get to choose when our hot flashes will occur. At a folk singer's concert, the performer enlisted the audience to sing the chorus midsong while she wiped her brow and carried them through with a few guitar chords. At the end of the song she announced, "I just had a hot flash." The audience broke into laughter and applause.

Hot flashes are not shameful events. They do not need to isolate or horrify us. They can and will happen wherever we are. They can be shared if we feel like sharing them. And, as Jane mentions above, we can see them as lighting the underlying changes we are making, as we go through our midlife exploration and reckoning.

I let my changes move through me like the weather.

Fear

Considering how dangerous everything is nothing is really very frightening.

GERTRUDE STEIN

Gertrude Stein's perspective on fear can both amuse us and help us, for it defies the notion that we need to be fearless to act. We do not. In fact, we rarely are fearless when we act. We simply learn to act by negotiating with our fear.

While it is important to respect danger and not to walk headlong into precarious situations, we have learned with age to better distinguish the real dangers from the imaginary ones. We have learned, too, the earmarks of our fear and how we tend to disguise it. Some of us flare with anger to cover up our fear; others withdraw and isolate. By recognizing the road map to our fear, we can locate our fear and address it more directly.

I acknowledge my fears today and act, not out of them, but alongside of them.

Clarity

Odder still how possessed I am with the feeling that now, aged 50, I'm just poised to shoot quite free straight & undeflected my bolts whatever they are.

VIRGINIA WOOLF

At fifty many of us mention this feeling of consolidation, of being ready to launch ourselves forth without the old constraints of youth. We have lived a half a century. If we have spent a lot of time and energy wading through the past, we are ready to put that behind us. We know what gives meaning to our lives, and we are going to have it.

Often when this new, more direct energy flows through us, we barely recognize it as ours at first. We have been taught as women to be more cautious than men, to equivocate and act as if we were unsure of ourselves. We have seen women who exhibit a straightforward, clear energy accused of being masculine. We have even seen them dyke-baited. But who cares? It is time for us to have our clarity and enjoy its expression. This energy is ours, and we are eager to grasp it. Having lived these first fifty years, we are going to have our due.

I won't have the clarity of my energy deflected by confusion.

Growth

Can it be that even as
one grows to fit the
space one lives in, one
cannot grow unless
there's space to grow?

RITA DOVE

We outgrow our clothes in childhood;
they must be replaced with larger ones.
Our body stops growing by a certain
age but our psyche continues to stretch
and burgeon, especially if we provide it
the space.

We know the feeling of being confined, of being too close
to another person or to people in a way that is stifling, of
needing elbow room or more space to breath. At the time of
our menopause, we need time and room to step back, away
from others, to take stock and tune in to the deep change
going on within us.

We return from our step back having opened new rooms
to fill. Perhaps a room with an altar for meditation. Perhaps a
room for fulfilling our creative self. Perhaps a room for reading what has always interested us.

*I give myself more elbow room and create space for
the directions in which I would like to grow.*

Shadow

If you have a skeleton in
your closet, take it out
and dance with it.

CAROLYN MCKENSIE

Don't be fooled by the appearances of others. Everyone has a skeleton in her closet. It's not so much what we try to hide as how we deal with it that makes the difference which allows us to live our lives expansively.

Having reached midlife, if we have danced *around* our skeletons, it is now time to dance *with* them. They may contain parts of our shadow self, which are difficult to embrace. Perhaps they are so-called negative feelings such as jealousy, envy, or rage. Perhaps it is time we knew more about the sources of these feelings so we can encounter the spooky secrets that have burdened us and free the hidden rooms within ourselves.

We want now to embrace all that is within us. We want to roam and range within without skirting barriers or bumping into locked closet doors.

I rejoice in the fact that I have nothing to hide.

Respect

The truth, above all, [is] that every human being deserves respect. We assert the respect due ourselves, when it is denied, through noncooperation; we assert the respect due others, through our refusal to be violent.

BARBARA DEMING

On the birthday of Martin Luther King, Jr., we contemplate the power of nonviolent resistance. Consciously or unconsciously many women have taken part in this mode of struggle. We have marched with our sisters to assert the respect due to us. We have marched to tell our government to cease building nuclear weapons, to end nuclear proliferation. We have seen major strides toward peace within our lifetimes.

We cannot truly respect ourselves without first respecting every other human being. For we are all connected, all part of one another. In our younger years, we might have thought the way to success was to leave others behind or to elevate ourselves by stepping on others. Through time and experience, we have discovered that the most important success occurs when we feel peace within, and this only occurs when no respect is denied, when we love ourselves and others. We do not need to step on anyone—our principles become our stairs.

Today, I appreciate the respect I offer all beings, including myself.

Perspective

In a single moment of our living, there is our ancestral and personal history, our future, even our death planted in us and already growing toward fulfillment.

LINDA HOGAN

Menopause is a good time to step back and gain perspective. We can become preoccupied with this moment and its discomforting changes, as if it is all we are made of. Or we can see ourselves in a larger picture, moving through a passage—moving from our original birth to a new birth, moving ultimately toward the fulfillment of our death.

When we see ourselves within the context of a lifetime, connected with our ancestors and all those who have touched us, we understand how much our lives have been guided by a force greater than our own wills, which think we must be in charge and cover all the bases. We are humbled and relieved when we are able to look at our lives from the long view.

I rest in the arms of the knowledge that I am an ever-growing spirit in every moment of my life.

Gestation

Energy deep within me is coming to a still-point in preparation for evoking my change.

FRANCES

The morning after a freshly fallen snow, a vision of pristine purity is shown to us. We see the beauty of color, from the blue of the sky against the white covering to the subtle reds of buds tightly closed, awaiting longer daylight before opening. The shadows of skeletal trees reflect on the snow. Time seems momentarily suspended.

Our menopause can be a winter, a time to be still against the hourly changing light. We hold ourselves through The Change, gestating parts of ourselves that we didn't know we possessed. We hold our bloods within, gestating our wisdom. We may feel turbulent with our hot flashes and moodiness, but we will embrace them, for it is our challenge to contain them and let them work their alchemy.

I stay in harmony with the gestation taking place within me.

Grief

> Sorrow is bound to death. Grief is bound to death. Each moment is not as fragile and fleeting as I once thought. Each moment is hard and lasting and so holds much that I must mourn for.
>
> **JAMAICA KINCAID**

As we grow older we come to understand that because a moment is impossible to capture, it is all the more precious and meaningful to live through. Once we might have dreaded involving ourselves with places we knew we were going to leave or with people we knew were going to die or otherwise depart. Now we realize that all of life is in constant flux. We do not seek security by trying to stabilize things around us; we seek it by accepting the nature of life and living in harmony with it.

We all feel grief at our losses although many of us try to avoid or deny it. Perhaps we are afraid to see death, to comprehend our mortality. Grief pursues us until we stop running and turn to face it. In this process we realize our own fragility and come to appreciate the joy of being present now.

Each moment behind me is gone. I grieve it and let it go.

Age-passing

There is strange reverse correlation with the actual demographic shift, as increasing millions now lived well beyond their sixties the proliferation of [TV] programs that dealt with the "problem" of age and the stepped-up sales pitch for products that promised to stop aging all underline the message that age was acceptable *only if it passed for emulated youth.*

BETTY FRIEDAN

We are all influenced by the media, as nearly every day we read a newspaper or magazine or watch TV. Here we find advertisers catering almost exclusively to the youth market, even though many of us in midlife have more disposable income than the young.

Why are we creating a society in which there is no respect for aging even as a greater percentage of the population is getting older? In which the singular compliment about aging is: "But you don't *look* forty . . . fifty . . . sixty . . . seventy"? Wouldn't midlife be rosier if we looked forward to the strengths and wonders that unfold in old age? But how are we to know them if they remain invisible?

This is a good time to alert our society to its false presentation of aging.

Today, I refuse to cooperate with the denigration of aging.

Envy

Finally, at fifty-five, I can
say I don't envy younger
women anymore.

SUSANNA

Ask a group of women over age forty-five how they honestly feel about younger women and many of them will say, "I hate them," "I don't trust anyone under forty," "I can't keep my eyes off them," "I want what they have," or "I can't bear to look at them." This is the nature of envy—attraction and repulsion for something we don't or can't have.

Rationally, we know there is no sense in trying to control age. Therefore we often deny these feelings of envy. However, feelings are not facts, and we might as well admit them. Our feelings of envy can help us to see what we have not been able to accept.

Furthermore, if our envy is not made conscious we are liable to act it out, competing with our daughters, racing to keep up with youth, or emulating youthful ways. Envy, when acknowledged, can often be transformed with a joke or carried along in a sidecar of awareness, but it ceases to have the power to poison or sabotage us.

Today, I let my envy show me the things I long for.

Reflection

I see myself in my friends and in the people I work with, not on Madison Avenue and certainly not in the movies. I look at my friends as we all crumble gracefully and find joy and power in that.

LACE JACKSON

Why frustrate ourselves looking for positive self-images in places where they are not to be found? Why compare our bodies to the smooth-skinned beauties in the movies or the models in the magazines, who don't look real anyway.

We all require reflection to see ourselves clearly. In a media-dominated culture, it is easy to forget that the prominent images parading before us are not comprehensive of reality. For more accuracy, let us look to friends who are more our age.

When we watch our friends, we do not see their surfaces change without also seeing the full breadth of their lives change. In this way we obtain a more accurate reflection.

I look at the many-faceted lives of my friends for reflection of myself at midlife.

Home

The journey brought me home, and at home I found myself a post-menopausal woman engaged in the tasks of the reincorporation phase: assimilation, inte-gration, and finding a way to share what I had experienced. . . . I found myself not in quest of home but: home.

CHRISTINE DOWNING

Christine Downing made a journey around the world to honor her midlife transition, and the journey brought her home. It was a place she had not even considered in the preparatory stage— a place of being "in tutelage to . . . Hestia," the Greek goddess of hearth and home.

How many of us have made and maintained a home for our families or for ourselves but still search for a sense of home—for the place that roots us so profoundly we feel grounded every day, for the place that holds us firmly in our center, for the place that brings all our separate parts under one roof?

Is not our longing for home a longing for integration of all that we are? Can we imagine finding such a rainbow on the other side of menopause? Let us anticipate our coming home with joy!

Each step in my quest for home brings me closer to that place.

Valuation

Why doesn't a 60 year old woman get the same respect as a 60-year-old oriental rug! How much longer must we all be stepped on before we're considered truly valuable?

SYBIL ADELMAN
SAGE

Older women in our culture have not been accorded proper respect. We must be willing to end our denial about this fact and start changing it. A first step is for us to begin to give that deserved respect to our women elders, but this will not come easy for we have long been trained to identify with youth.

Though one by one we ferret out certain older women to emulate and use as role models, we nonetheless elevate them to the pedestal of exceptions. This may help us, but it does not change the overall picture of aging women today. The time has come for us to take a bold stand, to fight against the culture's attitudes and begin the veneration of older women.

I create a new legacy about aging for my daughters and younger sisters by respecting and valuing older women and what they have to offer.

Fifty

I think it is important to say that 50 is not a delayed 40. . . . Let there be less marveling at our wonderful preservation and more respect for the maturity of our mind and spirit. . . . Fifty is 50, and to deny that is to deny wisdom, experience and life itself.

JANE O'REILLY

Once you've gotten there, you know how different fifty is from forty. Forty seems to be the age of a hazy awakening—"Okay, now, it's time to go for what is missing in my life." What is missing may be passion, or participation in more productive and satisfying work, or a void in the spiritual dimension. Many of us find our lives turned upside down at forty, driven by the awareness, conscious or not, that time is passing.

At fifty we look back on this previous decade with some compassion. We are old enough to receive its lessons. Our desire for a spiritual dimension, if we've developed and fed it, may have oriented us to new sources of satisfaction—an alignment with our sense of higher purpose, or a spiritual practice that brings us regular connection.

I trust that each age will bring to me all that it has to offer.

Osteoporosis

"Ah, yes," Grandmother Growth smiles rather wantonly, "it would do you well to develop a taste for dark greens tarted with vinegar and mated with garlic. These things will build a fine bone to support you as you become Crone."

**GRANDMOTHER GROWTH
(SUSUN S. WEED)**

One of the major appeals of Estrogen Replacement Therapy (ERT) for menopausal and post-menopausal women is that it reduces the rate of post-menopausal bone fractures. However, ERT must be taken consistently over a period of many years. Many of us are not able to use ERT because of our cancer histories, or even if we are, we prefer to seek more natural methods.

We can build and maintain strong bones to a good extent with diet. We need foods that supply us with adequate dietary calcium and a good climate for digestion (thus the vinegar). We need exercise such as walking, jogging, or lifting weights, exercise that specifically puts weight on our bones.

There are many fine resources today for learning how to give our bones their best chances to remain strong. What better investment could we make for our bodies than to become informed, and what better time will there ever be for making dietary changes than now, during our transformation?

Today, I invest in a commitment to diet and exercise.

Images of Middle Age

It really isn't the body—it is the replacement image. There is none. I'm not washed-up, at the end of my rope, over the hill, on the decline, or any of the other euphemisms, at least not overtly. But what am I?

JEWELLE GOMEZ

When we set aside all the useless euphemisms that float about us as we grow older, we are left in a vacuum. We don't want to simply rebel against these euphemisms because that only demonstrates we still believe in them enough to try and disprove them. Even those of us who have long rejected traditional perceptions of who we are have to confront this moment and, once more, create our own images to lead us forward.

One advantage to finding all the old notions unfit is that the field before us is wide open: to fill it, we must only free our imaginations. Our bodies are our guides. They slow us down, turn us inward, heat us for transition. Our spirits give us longing. If we listen to the longing, we are led to a deep but quiet voice within, one that can direct us.

Who do I want to be? If I can see that woman, I can be her.

Productivity

I expect to die, but I
don't plan to retire.

MARGARET MEAD

Accompanying our fear of midlife may be a doomsday anticipation of retirement, but we can assume Margaret Mead's attitude. Even if our job requires official retirement, we can anticipate this and segue into other productive activities, satisfying our desire to work.

One of the factors that contributes to longevity is the presence of organized, complex activity in our lives. This may be one reason we women outlive men. Some men, after retirement, tend not to fill their days with organized activity. Women, whose work has always transcended the strict dichotomy of home or office, are less likely to stop working even after retiring from a job.

Productive work is a boon to us all. It provides a sense of purpose and accomplishment. It provokes our minds and often extends our sense of community, providing new contexts for meeting people.

I envision a ripening productivity dispersed through my life, regardless of my age.

Rehearsal's Over

When one's young one doesn't feel a part of it yet. . . . Everything is in rehearsal. To be repeated ad lib, to be put right when the curtain goes up in earnest. One day you know that the curtain is up all the time. That was the performance.

SYBILLE BEDFORD

When do we realize the curtain is up? Not solely on one day, but in a moment here, a moment there, we suddenly become aware of ourselves fully in life. We lose the self-consciousness of looking over our shoulders, watching the rehearsal. This happens more and more in midlife until it is almost as if youth was the rehearsal.

To feel a part of life is to be living life more on its own terms. In youth we spend much of our energy rebelling, rejecting what others tell us. We don't like to have rules imposed on us, and yet we complain about them more often than we go about changing them. We feel more a part of life when we are able to see it from a broader view, gaining a picture of how we human beings fit into nature, how we can learn to live in harmony with it, and how our participation in life influences its course. We are neither insignificant nor at the center.

I am part of life. I see my true relation to it.

Innocence Lost

I'd already received the image that humanity, having left the innocence of the Garden of Eden in order to gain the wisdom of experience, would return to that garden to integrate the wisdom with innocence, the body with the spirit, and create a physical paradise on Earth.

SHAKTI GAWAIN

Perhaps this broad journey that Shakti Gawain envisions humanity to be taking is also mirrored separately in each of us as we encounter our midlife. We have left the innocence of youth to receive some of the painful knocks of experience, also finding opportunities along the way to express our passion and receive our share of joy.

Now our job is to integrate wisdom with innocence. Many of us have become jaded. We may have adopted indifference as a shield, pretending not to care about things that may be lost in the future. But this attitude deprives us of our passion as well. We must find our innocent, eager self and bring her forth so that she can be side by side with the wisdom of our life experience.

I put my experience to better use than to simply let it make me feel jaded.

Discipline

How we spend our days is, of course, how we spend our lives. What we do with this hour, and that one, is what we are doing. A schedule defends from chaos and whim.

ANNIE DILLARD

Especially as we reach midlife, we are likely to become more aware of the "unlived life" in us—the art we always meant to make after we became more secure, the neglected work or career we always intended to pursue, the more pensive life we always meant to slow down for.

This is a good time to take stock and ask: Are we doing what we want to with our hours? Have we learned to achieve the discipline of a balanced schedule—one that alleviates chaos and still permits spontaneity?

As we discover the things we would like to be doing but haven't done yet, this is a good time to take steps to change how we spend our hours, knowing this will add up to a change in our lives.

Now is the right time to enjoy my hours by fulfilling my directions and desires.

Listening

And—teach us to
   listen!—
We can hear it in water,
   in wood,
and even in stone.
We are earth of this
   earth, and we
are bone of its bone.

BARBARA DEMING

In our midlife years we want to grow quiet and listen. We want to hear the instructions coming from our bodies as they go through the natural course of change. We want to hear the earth and be at peace with it.

In our confusion about the changes of midlife, we may need to journey to the top of a mountain and listen to the wind and the wood and the stone. We must come to a still-point, releasing all the chatter of inner voices. Then we can truly hear the earth and our bodies.

This day, Groundhog Day, Candlemas Day—the midpoint between winter solstice and spring equinox—marks the light returning and the beginning of our turning back outward from our inner transformation. It is a good day to go to the top of the mountain and listen.

I listen to the earth and know I am of it.

Perimenopause

One winter at forty-eight, precipitated by a stressful shock, my periods stopped for three months without warning. I never thought I'd long for a period, but I mourned every time I opened the bathroom closet and saw the box of tampons.

GINGER

In perimenopause, or the early stages of menopause, periods become sporadic and often change character. We become acutely aware of the loss of regularity, since we still expect that the next period will surely come in twenty-eight days or twenty-four days or whatever our cycle has been. After six or eight weeks we may begin to wonder if the last one was *the* last one. Then when the next one does come, we have a feeling of wonder, perhaps similar to the awe of the twelve- or thirteen-year-old encountering her earliest periods. Knowing it will end soon, we want to grasp this experience. Just what has been its influence on us? Will we have any memory for the physical feelings of our periods once they are gone? With each menstrual period we become more acutely aware of womb, of fullness, but also of vulnerability within. Now that we have an awareness of imminent movement toward the other side of The Change, it is strange to realize our months will no longer be sequenced with these markers.

I appreciate the heightened awareness that comes with impending loss.

Compassion

Compassion for oneself and others opens the door to grace, to a spiritual dimension of existence that includes and transcends everyday routine. The problem for a woman is that she has been taught to feel compassion for someone else: a child, a friend, a lover, a husband, a parent, or for suffering humanity.

VIRGINIA BEANE RUTTER

Menopause is a good time to remember, or perhaps to fully realize for the first time, that compassion for oneself is essential. This lesson is timely because the vulnerability of change may bring out more neediness in us. The symbolic moving into a second adulthood may provoke the child within us to feel as if she is being left behind unless we attend to her with compassion. And she is often the figure who needs compassion most—because of the wounds she suffered at too early an age to be equipped to handle them.

Turning the light of compassion upon ourselves may not come easy. It may show us pain that we have wished to avoid. It may light up a deep sadness. But it is by allowing ourselves to feel this suffering within us that we come to wholeness and feel grace.

Today, I extend compassion to myself.

Truth

What would happen if one woman told the truth about her life? The world would split open

MURIEL RUKEYSER

We often find that telling the truth about our lives splits the world open. The truth about midlife for women has been hidden under the negative imagery surrounding menopause and the dread of aging in our culture.

We come to this time in our lives with the advantage of having learned twenty years ago to look through our own eyes at our real experience and to tell it to others. And when we do this now, we discover there is much to find agreeable about midlife. We have grown into ourselves, we have less fear of others, and we express ourselves more readily. There is discomfort, too. We do not particularly enjoy our night sweats or hot flashes, our turbulence of mood or depression. But if we are aware of the full landscape of our life changes, these discomforts do not need to be the centerpiece of our transformation.

I speak the full truth of my life, and speak it again and again to my sisters and daughters.

Change

If my life changes, I can't go back and dig up what was once real to me.

JUDITH JAMISON

The one thing we can be sure of is that life does change—we have dynamic, regenerating bodies that lose old cells and create new ones every day. We also seem naturally inclined to want to hang on tight to anything that has served us well or given us enjoyment. However, in midlife we discover that the very same things that satisfy one year often cease to satisfy in the next. This leaves us with nostalgia.

Nostalgia can provide a pleasant escape from the present, floating us back to the past. However, it does little to fulfill our present needs. When we stop longing for what's gone, we are still faced with taking action to provide ourselves with what we need today.

We fear change, yet how would our lives be without it? Change offers us continual renewal and the excitement of discovery.

I appreciate the opportunity to let go of the old and flow with the changes of the present.

Direction

It was . . . an injunction laid on all of us, not just the talented, to follow the trajectory chance and fate have launched on us, like a poet keeping faith with his muse.

MARY MCCARTHY

A poet trusts that her muse is revealing the poem to her. She becomes a responsive ear and takes pen to paper to record what she hears. We all have a path to follow, a voice to hear. We cannot be truly centered within ourselves unless we are listening and responding.

Midlife is a time when the need to feel we are in harmony with whatever greater design exists becomes more urgent for us. We want to further develop and utilize our talents. We want to allow ourselves seriousness of purpose. We want to know that the actions of our lives touch the lives of others and have influence in the collective course of the evolution of humankind.

If we have spent much of our youth very self-focused, we may want to turn outward and comprehend more fully how we fit in the world.

My path is unique. I deepen my commitment to following it.

Rituals

A profoundly spiritual ritual may have nothing to do with otherworldliness at all, but may celebrate the sacredness of the real and the natural: women, earth, flesh, daily living, human relationships.

BARBARA G. WALKER

Ritual is a form of acknowledgment or validation that can be done alone or in groups. Ritual can help provide a clear-cut moment, marking when old clothes are left behind and new ones are donned, when we are realigned in our relationship to the earth, or when we come in tune with the energy of the season.

Ritual is a resource that can bond and empower us. We can develop our own rituals to suit our needs exactly. If we are having a difficult time with our menopause, each day we might spend a few ritual moments lighting a candle and letting ourselves focus on this passage. We might carry a small stone in our pocket when we are frightened or lonely, designating it as a piece of earth to ground us. We might use each of our hot flashes as a moment to say: *Yes, change, I hear you.*

Small rituals offer me a chance to tap greater powers.

Ignorance

It is not knowing, maybe more than anything, that holds women in the grip of fear. Had I known at the time that the physical problems I am experiencing were classic signs of menopause, I could have saved the time, money, and grief of visiting doctors.

LONNIE BARBACH, PH.D.

Dread of menopause has kept us from recognizing its first signs, which seem vague and shadowy but become readily more distinct with knowledge. For instance, sleep disturbances may be caused by an alteration in FST (a follicle-stimulating hormone). An increase of this hormone, in an effort to stimulate the release of an egg, causes a certain activity in the brain that results in less REM, or dream, sleep. When one is deprived of dream sleep, one feels tired and cranky.

Medical science, functioning from a disease orientation, has tended to confine the definition of menopause to its most dramatic year or so of change—the first year of no periods—paying little attention to the perimenopausal years. Many of us go on expensive medical searches for the causes of our problems when, at forty-eight or forty-nine, we have months of poor sleep, depression, fatigue, or other perimenopausal symptoms. While there are other diseases or problems that might be the cause of our symptoms, menopause should be at the top of the list of possibilities, but often it is not.

I take responsibility for educating myself about menopause.

The Present

I make my greatest
contribution to the
future by being fully
here in the present.

CAMILLE

Most of us dream that one day we will be seen as important, as having made a significant contribution, as having reached some pinnacle of achievement that marks us with distinction. In reality the distinction in our lives is marked by how we are taking part in the present.

If we ignore our current relationship to the earth, our children and grandchildren may be paying our debts long after we are gone. If we work now to right the things we see awry, our efforts will add up to an evolution for the future.

Look at the people we hold up as heroes: Eleanor Roosevelt, Amelia Earhart, Rosa Parks, Martin Luther King, Jr. They did not wait to step into the future. They stepped into the now.

Today, I bring my full force to the present, letting go of the temptation to wait for the future.

Time

I must govern the clock,
not be governed by it.

GOLDA MEIR

The vantage point of midlife lets us look back over the years that have marched by. We probably remember some joy even in our most difficult years. We may also see how futile our efforts to worry life along in a particular direction have been.

Our fear is self-centered and keeps us from seeing the ever-comforting effect of the passage of time. For time always lends the next lesson. Time always restores the warmth in our hearts after they have been broken. Time always offers us wisdom.

I let go of my fears and let time be my healer.

Living Today

This is my life. Each hour is a possibility not to be banked. These days are not a preparation for living, some necessary but essentially extraneous divergence from the main course of my living. They are my life. . . . It is the consciousness of this that gives a marvelous breadth to everything I do consciously.

AUDRE LORDE

Those who live with a terminal illness develop a keen awareness of the futility of waiting to live the unlived life. Time may not last for them. Or for us. If we are still preparing for the time of our "real" life, we had best begin living our real life now.

Many of us find that, at least in certain areas of our lives, we arrive at midlife acting as if we've not yet come into full entitlement for living. Gradually a new awareness dawns. We are no longer in that youthful time, waiting to come to a ripening. We are in the ripening time.

When we live as if each day might be our last, we come to know the wealth available in each hour, each feeling, each exchange with another. Our appetite is satisfied for we are filled with our own vitality.

I live today as today, banking nothing on tomorrow.

Integrity

What is it we see in the eyes of someone who lives their life with integrity? It's easier to say what's missing—the sense of unspoken apology, the fear, the need for pretense.

BONNIE MYOTAI TREACE

Integrity means wholeness. We cannot be whole without looking into ourselves and recognizing what Jung called our shadow—the dark side that we often prefer to project onto others. Our shadow contains our repressed energies, which are often those feelings we consider negative, such as anger, sadness, jealousy, envy. As we grow older and are able to look at these feelings, to take them in and own them, we can see how they make a contribution to our wholeness.

When we are at one with ourselves and our universe, our eyes look clearly and directly into the eyes of others. We do not need to judge, nor do we become easily heckled when others judge us. We know who we are. Our sense of purpose and direction is in sync with the will of our higher selves. This gives us a quiet but reliable and powerful energy.

Today, I notice the moments when integrity shines through my eyes.

Love

I'd rather have roses on
my table than diamonds
on my neck.

EMMA GOLDMAN

Flowers on the table are an expression of love and of life. They are living beings standing in witness of us as we gaze upon them. Other riches fail to satisfy if we feel our life is loveless.

Valentine's Day presents us with an opportunity to be aware of those we love and to express that love. If we do not have a sweetheart, we may feel sad about this and jealous of those who do, but we can also look a little further to notice that we are loved by plenty of people.

In midlife, some of us who are not coupled yearn deeply for that primary connection, while others, after long struggles with a relationship or relationships, may be very content to be alone. Let us respect our desires. Let us shamelessly acknowledge that our first priority is to love ourselves.

I give myself flowers as a declaration of my love for me.

Memory

Memory is a story we make
up from snatches of the past.

LYNNE SHARON SCHWARTZ

Isn't it amazing how differently an incident from the past is remembered by two people? One event can create many stories, and we create the one that tells of our perspective.

The older we grow the more we seem to want to use our memory to place the events of our lives into a coherent story. Perhaps our story tells how we ventured forth urgently in youth, seeking to find ourselves, and how we thought the world was ours when we enjoyed some early successes. Then we encountered some falls and felt discouragement, but ultimately this served to give us the grace of a deeper understanding of ourselves and others.

In our midlife, perimenopausal years we may find our memory for details floundering. This can be upsetting, as if it forebodes the further potential memory losses of old age. But there is comfort in the notion that we are becoming more selective in all areas. We are of an age to be more deliberate with our energies. Our memory, too, wants to narrow and focus on what is most important.

*I trust my memory to remember the story that
provides a reliable foundation for me.*

Emergence

Maybe being myself is
always an acquired taste.

PATRICIA HAMPL

Becoming ourselves is a mission that engages us for a lifetime. While we are born into ourselves, we are also born into a family from which we are somewhat indistinguishable in our early years. And we are born into a community with rules, restrictions, and a collective identity.

The process of uncovering our particular individual nature is a gradual one. Much of this learning is still taking place in midlife. For years, many of us have lived the roles of wife and/or mother, and with the departure of our children, our midlife provides an opportunity to discover and give expression to other aspects of ourselves.

We may not even recognize ourselves when we first venture forth, uncovering and focusing on what has been denied or hidden. But with time we recognize and love the emergence of this being.

I treasure the emergence of myself.

Vitality

People . . . may be vital or still, may be radiant or dull, may be free or bound. We may choose to develop our life energy, our self-direction, our joy in being, that is, we may live a life of spirit, or we may be bound to a terrible self-created confinement.

SHEILA RUTH

As we age we become more of who we are. If we are women who have developed our spirits, we will continue to expand to greater joy, rocked of course by the angst that also comes with a full life. If we have not developed our spirits, we will constrict further and further, moving with a narrow view and bound where we might be free.

Whatever way we have lived up until now, midlife presents a chance for us to redirect ourselves toward the care and nurturance of our spirit. How do we begin to do this? Often with a simple action—a commitment to a yoga class, an experiment in meditation, giving ourselves a daily quiet hour, taking a journey to a place that beckons.

When we tend our spirit we are rewarded with vitality. Like a horse free in the pasture, we discover that we are complete and free to run as we please.

Today, I tend to my spirit.

Discovery

Writing fiction has developed in me an abiding respect for the unknown in a human lifetime and a sense of where to look for the threads, how to follow, how to connect, find in the thick of the tangle what clear line persists. The strands are all there: to the memory nothing is ever really lost.

EUDORA WELTY

We each find our own way, making the connections that bring our lives together. Especially as we come into midlife, we develop a respect and even an awe for the mysterious process of discovery.

We have crossed so many intersections by now, deciding to go left, go right, go straight ahead. How have we known in the "thick of the tangle" which direction to take? Sometimes we have called on counselors or friends for guidance. Sometimes we have followed our intuition. Sometimes we have cast ourselves into a more serendipitous state, wanting the wind to choose for us by blowing us down one path or another. No path is an error—though some we experience as detours.

My way opens before me as I follow my intuition and my guides.

Goddesses Within

Midlife may bring a
new configuration of
goddesses, or the new
prominence of one
goddess. This potential
shift happens at every
major new stage of life.

**JEAN SHINODA
BOLEN, M.D.**

Jean Shinoda Bolen shows us how we
are aligned with the energies of a particular goddess or series of goddesses,
using the goddesses from the Greek
pantheon—such as Hestia, the hearth
builder, Demeter, the mother goddess,
and Aphrodite, the creator and the ex-
presser of the erotic. Knowledge of these
archetypes can help us see our own energies as a part of a
larger, universal pool, and we may be less surprised when new
and different energies emerge from us.

As we enter a new stage of life, we find it hard to recognize ourselves as we express new energies. Perhaps we feel a
surge of creative juices, or a mothering instinct reemerges just
in time to nurture and help take care of our grandchildren.

Today, I relate to the changing configuration of the
goddesses within me.

Winter

Who can bear another
storm, another freezing
day or night? I can't.

FREIDA

In northern climates, winter tries us.
Even if we like it and greet it gleefully,
by this time of year our tolerance wears
thin. Our cells begin to crave more light
and the stronger sunshine of spring. Like an addict, we are
not satisfied with small, incremental doses. When February
offers a warm day or two and then plunges us deeper than
ever back into winter, we are especially dismayed.

Menopause is like the winter season of our bodies,
despite the heat that often accompanies it. It, too, tries us.
We wish for a faster transition and discover our wishes mean
nothing at all. When we are faced with the feeling that we
can't bear for it to continue, we must seek a peaceful way to
go on. This way is acceptance—to choose peace rather than
the turmoil of trying to change the unchangeable. We only
need to seek this day by day.

*As soon as I accept the current conditions, I discover
I can go on.*

Purpose

We've buried so many people we've loved; that is the hard part of living this long. Most everyone we know has turned to dust. Well, there must be some reason we're still here. That's why we agreed to do this book; it gives us a sense of purpose.

SARAH DELANEY

Sarah and Bessie Delaney wrote their stories in *Having Our Say* at the ages of 100 and 102. They inspire us with their down-to-earth humor, their practical and humble attitudes toward life, and their vital longevity.

Images of strong old women are not easy to come by in our culture. We think far more often of the old women who blankly shuffle up and down the corridors of nursing homes than we do of those who continue to manage on their own, helping out their neighbors and friends. This despite the fact that only about 7 percent of the elderly population is residing in nursing homes.

A sense of purpose is a deep motivator. In midlife, by getting more in touch with our purpose, we begin to see our lives open to the unexpected and the sublime, and we are grateful for the time we have left.

A sense of purpose tells me why I am here.

Solitude

Long ago the word *alone* was treated as two words, *all one*. To be *all one* meant to be wholly one, to be in oneness either essentially or temporarily. That is precisely the goal of solitude, to be all one. It is the cure for the frazzled state so common to modern woman, the one that makes her, as the old saying goes, "leap onto her horse and ride off in all directions."

CLARISSA PINKOLA ESTÉS, PH.D.

We need solitude to experience the gift of being one unto ourselves. We must distinguish this from isolation—the impulse to retreat from our connections with others, which is also a retreat from ourselves. When we create solitude, we come forward to meet our being.

Midlife may be the first chance for many of us to spend any considerable time alone. We may have had children in our house for years. We may have worked obsessively in every spare hour. Now it is our time to sometimes be alone and recognize ourselves *as one*. This idea may present itself as frightening. After all, what if we stand still and discover we have to confront our feeling that there is no one home inside us?

No one home is a starting point for becoming *all one*. Let us begin with honesty and find ourselves filling up.

I choose solitude today as a chance to appreciate the oneness of my being.

Autonomy

I am learning to be complete unto myself and appreciate that which surrounds me without needing to be it. Like any art, the creation of self is both natural and seemingly impossible. It requires training as well as magic.

HOLLY NEAR

The creation of self is a delicate art. We find ourselves in great part by being closely connected with other human beings. We form ourselves a little here, a little there, taking in from the examples of others, listening to an inner voice that confirms what is ours. We seek and find our pleasures at the same time that we discover what pains us.

Perhaps love might be defined as the appreciation of the essence of a being. To love another we need to be able to love ourselves and claim our own autonomy. We need to be able to relate to someone else while leaving them to be who they are.

My autonomy is both complete and within a circle of other beings.

Anger

Although feminists early discovered that the private is the public, women's exercise of power and control, and the admission and expression of anger necessary to that exercise, has until recently been declared unacceptable.

CAROLYN G.
HEILBRUN

Can a woman express her anger? Anger goes with being human and is as natural as joy, but we have been socialized to hide our anger, to bury it under silent resentment, or to express it only against ourselves. It is an emotion that provides distance, a step back from the person or incident that provokes it. Anger lets us know when our toes have been stepped on. It lets us know when and where we need to push back.

We who are entering midlife today are fortunate enough to be of a generation of women who've begun to recognize and exercise their anger. If we do not like the images being handed down to us about this phase of our lives, we do not need to consume them. Instead, let us protest them. Let us use our anger as the fire to ignite us. Let us appreciate how the expression of our anger can create change.

Today, I allow my anger to fuel me.

Wise Old Woman

An archetype is an inherited, preformed image that is a composite of a certain set of attributes. We have many of these archetypes or characters in our unconscious. One of them is the *Wise Old Woman.*

DIANE MARIECHILD

Who do we see when we contemplate the Wise Old Woman? Do we see a primitive creature, a woman with wild hair and long, fanglike teeth living in a cave? We may well see this ancient woman who cares nothing for refinement, for she exists in the collective imagination. We may see a modern grandmother, our own or someone we have not known but whose strength we can feel.

Contemplating an image of the Wise Old Woman may help us to contact the wise old woman within us. She is there for each of us. We may have long shunned the very notion of her, and consequently, she may respond to us now with guarded reluctance. But by giving her our attention, we stir up her presence in us.

The Wise Old Woman can guide us through menopausal changes. She has the guts to help us shake loose from old notions and realign our values.

I visualize the Wise Old Woman within me and seek her guidance.

Mother Nature

Nature, since it has mothered all, may be regarded as Mother Nature. Only those who understand Mother Nature, will understand her many children. If we choose to avoid mistakes and desire to have a wise guide throughout life, we should study the wisdom of Mother Nature's ways.

MERLIN STONE

There is always a lesson before us laid out by Mother Nature. We only need to take a walk to find it. Discouraged by the length of winter in northern climates, we may come upon pussy willows blooming with new life this month, reminding us of the imminent renewal of spring. Watching the snow thaw and rush through streams and rivers to fill the reservoirs, we are reassured by the cycle of Mother Nature. The very same snow that got in our way and was a nuisance now provides us with an abundant supply of water.

Through Mother Nature we see the larger picture of our needs and her provisions. She shows us our short-sighted tendencies. In midlife her cyclical nature helps us to have patience with our changing bodies.

Mother Nature is my guide. I honor and study her.

Struggle

> Nothing, I am sure, calls forth the faculties so much as the being obliged to struggle with the world.
>
> **MARY WOLLSTONECRAFT**

Struggle is ill-appreciated. Rarely do we thank it. Instead we implore: Why is my life so difficult? Why am I not given a less bumpy road to travel? Now that I am in midlife, shouldn't I be able to sail unhindered?

How much of ourselves would we know if we had never had to struggle? How many of our resources would lie dormant? How often would we have stretched our limits only to surpass them?

Midlife and menopause are a struggle for many women. We must struggle with the foregone images planted in us about aging. Some of us struggle with the physical changes. Some of us face a spiritual bankruptcy that leaves us empty and yearning to find fulfillment. Let us be mindful of the gift and potency of our struggle—it draws forth parts of us we have perhaps not even known were ours.

I see my struggles in a positive light today.

Death

So we die before our own eyes; so we see some chapters of our lives come to their natural end.

SARAH ORNE JEWETT

We fear death, thinking we know nothing of it, thinking it is the one unknowable event. Yet we see it occur daily in nature; we even see it occur in ourselves as we move through life's stages.

We experience a feeling of death when we shed an old way of being that no longer serves us. We hold fast to it as long as possible before we release it to the wind and mourn its loss. Then we take our fill of the new way of being that becomes possible.

We lose people we love deeply; they die, or sometimes we grow apart. At the time of such an occurrence, the loss may feel unnatural, but eventually we come to see that it is natural. Eventually we see this chapter come to a close before our very eyes. We see, too, the births that grow from the deaths.

I mourn my little deaths and take the fill of their experience.

Empowerment

Let woman then go on—not asking favors, but claiming as a right the removal of all hindrances to her elevation in the scale of being—let her receive encouragement for the proper cultivation of all her powers, so that she may enter profitably into the active business of life.

LUCRETIA MOTT

We have struggled in our younger years to claim our right to "enter profitably into the active business of life." Now we struggle to bring our full feisty selves into our middle-aged years of wisdom, against the grain of a society that still cultivates youthful beauty as a standard for the valuation of women.

Who will encourage us in the cultivation of our powers? *We will.* As we support and validate each other, we grow in strength and visibility. Our presence encourages other women our age to be at peace with acting and looking their ages. The more we stay present with our reality, the more gifts this offers us.

The "active business of life" at this stage includes reining in our various aspects—such as what we have learned of human nature, our talents as we have developed them, our commitment to certain principles—and integrating them powerfully.

I take advantage of my right to cultivate my full powers.

Myth

[Mythical] images hold profound revelations of humanity's mental and emotional development. For example, body and world stand for each other so consistently in the mythological mode that every tale of doomsday can be seen to allegorize the terrifying dissolution of the self in death, while every creation demonstrably presents a buried memory of birth.

BARBARA G. WALKER

The myth of Inanna shows us a midlife journey. We see a woman who, though she has all that she could want in the upperworld, decides to go to the underworld to unite with her sister, the Queen of the Underworld, in order to find herself more deeply. In her descent, she must divest herself of all material possessions. She removes her clothing and her jewelry. She enters the underworld naked and bowed low.

Inanna approximates a death in the underworld; then through the intervention of humble servants, she is able to make an ascent. But in order for her to be released from the underworld, she must choose someone else to return to the underworld in her stead.

The maturation we come to in midlife demands that we make choices in order to know ourselves more completely. Of the many ways to go, we must search in our depths, choose the right one for us, and let the others fall away.

The wisdom expressed in myths can guide and inform me.

Acceptance

I like trees because they seem more resigned to the way they have to live than other things do.

WILLA CATHER

Trees are not restless. They are rooted deeply in the place where they are born. They seem to be content to live a lifetime with the same neighbors. They encounter the seasons without complaint, contracting when appropriate, expanding and displaying their splendor when the season for new growth comes.

By contrast we are afflicted with longings that trees do not appear to have. Often we feel that our deep yearning for connection with others and with ourselves is not being satisfied. It makes us hunger for more so that we will be filled up.

Perhaps a tree can provide us with a calming example of acceptance. The more we accept and appreciate what we have, the less we focus on what we do not.

Today, I have all I need to find satisfaction.

Cost of Living

In spite of the cost of
living, it's still popular.

KATHLEEN NORRIS

It takes time to realize the cost of living and then some more time to accept it. By midlife we are placed at a vantage point for acceptance. We have encountered our share of heartaches and seen others have theirs. We realize that not only do bad things happen to good people, bad things happen to *all* people. We realize it is not what happens to us but how we handle it that counts.

Perhaps we have gone through bad times when the cost of living already seemed too high. We felt we had been dealt a bad hand. But we watched with inspiration how others around us handled their difficulties, and we began to understand that if someone offered us the chance to put our problems in a big pot and take back someone else's, we would probably prefer to keep our own.

Once we acknowledge that our problems do not victimize us, we can approach them with patience and fortitude and appreciate how much they have contributed to forming us.

Everything costs; every effort pays.

Sadness

Those who do not know how to weep with their whole heart don't know how to laugh either.

GOLDA MEIR

Sadness is a part of the human condition. We know it well by midlife. We also know what happens when we try to avoid it—it only grows, swelling under the cover we have placed over it, until misery pervades our entire being.

When we weep with our whole heart, we are allowing ourselves to feel pain and express it. We are allowing ourselves to have a heart, a full heart, even when our heart feels broken. This is an embrace of our pain. We often fear that when we allow our tears to flow freely we will go on crying forever. But our actual experience of granting this full expression is that we are soon finished crying and hope begins to shine through.

Joy comes to us not because we have no sadness but because we know our sadness and have given it its due. From our open heart laughter soon comes, showing us that we are traveling in the light.

I release my sadness and find laughter.

Life as Teacher

Fortunately [psycho-analysis] is not the only way to resolve inner conflicts. Life itself still remains a very effective therapist.

KAREN HORNEY

We live in an age of therapy, and many of us are greatly helped by seeking professionals for counseling. Yet let us not forget that life is ultimately our most consistent teacher. This is one reason that midlife excites us. We have accumulated quite a bit of experience in living. We have come to recognize our own outline. We know when we are lost, and we know how to find ourselves again.

Those inner conflicts we have not yet resolved regularly present themselves. Sometimes we walk right by them without even noticing. Eventually we are ready to see them, and there they are, staring us in the face. By admitting their existence we take the first step toward resolution. This takes us to the next step. If we keep on walking with them, eventually we will see our way to resolving them.

I embrace life as my teacher today and every day.

Contributions

> When you cease to make
> a contribution you begin
> to die.
>
> **ELEANOR ROOSEVELT**

The older we grow, the more wisdom and guidance we have to offer others—if we are willing to share what we have learned. And why wouldn't we? What can be the benefit of hoarding? There is none, and yet we may find within us the tendency not to share. Are we afraid we will become empty if we don't keep our knowledge to ourselves? Contrary to this impulse, we actually find that when we give of our wisdom generously, our well is filled anew.

If we feel depressed about our midlife, we might reorient our attitude by taking a look at our contributions. Are we actively contributing to righting the things we find wrong in the world—both in our personal world and in the larger world? Are we putting our talents to good use? Do we participate in our community in a way that serves others, not just ourselves?

Making a contribution gives us an active stance from which to feel alive and well. It is always an opportunity to grow and flourish.

My contributions repay me generously.

Pain

After great pain, a
formal feeling comes.

EMILY DICKINSON

Pain is a catalyst for the deep changes we make within us—the acceptance of injurious incidents in our past, the letting go of self-destructive behaviors that only hold us static and frustrate us, the discipline of seeking and sticking to a new way of doing things.

What is this feeling that comes following great pain? Perhaps it is a tranquility and sense of the beauty within us like a rainbow that appears after a storm. We are washed clean and ready for the new. We have been jumbled in the chaos of our pain, and now it is as if our cells have realigned themselves to settle in a new order.

We feel formal whenever new aspects of us are emerging. We do not yet have a strong familiarity with them. Who is she, we wonder, this woman who speaks out so directly about her feelings, or this woman who carries herself as if she deserves the best of everything, and as a result, often gets it.

I walk tall with the formal feeling of introducing my new self to the world.

Freedom

While we live in community and need
to comply with certain common rules,
we also need to think for ourselves.
Being resistant to all authority, disagree-
ing with every restraint that comes along, is not freedom; it is
rebellion. Constant rebellion keeps us locked to the power of
collective forces just as surely as mindless obedience does.

Freedom lies in our full expression of ourselves, which
means we must explore and get to know ourselves. Then we
must permit ourselves to show who we are. If we are hiding
behind a mask, we do not know freedom.

Out of our wish to belong, we often follow the impulse to
think the same as others. Freedom comes when we don't
need to do this. Especially by midlife, our years tell us to trust
and go from our own ideas. We need neither follow nor rebel.

Today, I step into the open meadow of freedom.

Anger

People who fight fire with fire
usually end up with ashes.

ABIGAIL VAN BUREN

It is wise to know and honor our anger but also to express it with self-restraint. By midlife we begin to learn this lesson. We have ended up too often with nothing but ashes.

Anger makes us bristle and step back, or it gives us the impulse to strike out and hurt the one who provokes us. These responses are quite natural. But as mature adults we are capable of exerting some restraint over these impulses without denying their existence. With time and more perspective, we can better understand the feelings that have been triggered in us. Then we are prepared to enter into a dialogue with the provoker, which will hopefully allow an expression of our anger that does not attempt to obliterate the other but remains within the bounds of respectful interaction.

*I neither deny my anger nor let it run riot
and rule me.*

Writing

It is my notebook that keeps me above the surface of the waters.

ANNA TSETSAEYVA

Journal writing gives voice to our experience as we go through transitions. As we record our understandings of events our words move some of our more unconscious motives into the light of consciousness. And from this new perspective we are able to see further.

Thoughts and feelings flash through our minds, racing around, making us feel at times as if we are squirrels on a turning wheel. We can intercept obsessive thinking by writing down our thoughts.

Writing also helps us hear ourselves, and who else is more important to listen to? Especially when we are in a dark passageway, the concreteness of words can be an anchor as we move haltingly forward.

Words can give form to my experience.

Humor

You grow up the day you have your first real laugh—at yourself.

ETHEL BARRYMORE

Being able to laugh at oneself is the gift of perspective. We are often so deeply focused on our problems and disasters that we allow no chance for looking at them through a slightly slanted lens. A slanted lens will reveal the fact that we are floundering but lovable humans, unable to escape our imperfections.

Laughing at our own foibles is a mark of maturity. Our laughter recognizes both our limits and our efforts to be limitless. Even though it doesn't attempt to change our behavior, laughter can help break us of obsessive, unfruitful patterns.

All laughter contributes to our well-being. There is acceptance at the bottom of it. And with acceptance comes hope.

I appreciate the restorative power of laughing at myself.

Fear

I think the moment when I discovered that everybody was afraid was a turning moment for me because I no longer had to worry about appearing fearful.

LUCILLE CLIFTON

How often we discover that others are afraid, too. And yet do we use this knowledge, like Lucille Clifton, to cease covering up our own fear? Or do we forget and continue to conceal our fear behind a mask?

As we come into our midlife years let us reward ourselves by allowing our own fears to be acknowledged and expressed. Then our fear will not be standing in our way or taking over our actions unconsciously. Nor will we have the stress of maintaining a false appearance.

Our fear need not stop us from entering any realm that we desire. When we walk hand in hand with it, we may walk more slowly and cautiously, but we will move forward, and no part of us will be left behind.

I recognize the fearful part in myself and in others.

Grief

Grief never leaves you
where it finds you.

GRANDMA MAC

Grief is a process that shakes us down. It is not one particular feeling but a turbulent ride through many aches, memories, impulses to clutch, and impulses to let go. No wonder we are confused by it.

We grieve not only our loved ones who die. We grieve a place we have to move from, relationships that flounder and die, and stages of life we leave behind. Rather than encounter the feelings of grief and loss, we sometimes try to remain in the past. If we have lost a parent, for instance, we may unconsciously try to become more like them to avoid having to separate from them. But this only causes us to become bogged down until eventually we are forced to face our loss.

When we come out the other side of grief, we are not quite the same person. We are washed clean by our turbulent journey. We come to accept the laws of Nature and to find out more about ourselves.

I surrender to my grief today.

Risk

What you risk reveals
what you value.

**JEANETTE
WINTERSON**

Would you risk an established, steady relationship for a wild attraction to a new love? Would you risk a secure job to develop talents you've allowed to lie dormant? Would you risk revealing your feelings even though you know they may upset the balance of a relationship?

We are confronted every day with choices that give our lives direction. These choices involve risks and are always decided according to our values. Sometimes this is hard to believe. If we have not placed value on certain aspects of ourselves, we may surprise ourselves when we suddenly choose to value them, though that path takes us away from security, for instance. Yet in time we discover that we were desperately in need of honoring another value—perhaps the value of deeper self-exploration or the value of discovering a more passionate self.

*Risks are choices that bring me to the edge of myself
and make me stretch.*

Dignity

There are some things we do simply because the doing is a success. We try to treat people fairly; we try to live our lives with dignity; we try, in our hearts and minds, to "go boldly where no man has gone." And isn't that the ultimate contribution we make to the human experiment?

NIKKI GIOVANNI

The human spirit seems to be a noble one to its core. We want to contribute. We want to see humankind go further toward realizing itself. We want to see ourselves become better people.

Sometimes social and political forces move us further away from this desire. We become caught up in material achievement or the striving for individual recognition, or we become stalled in preoccupation with our own personal problems. Midlife is a time for broad assessment and reorganization. Let us use this time to focus on our dignity.

When we are treating others fairly and not using anyone, we find the dignity in our being.

Today, noticing the simple dignity of how I breathe the life force into and out of my being, I appreciate the gift of my existence and the merits of my good behavior

Memory

> Memory magnifies, gathers light from tiny sources as the eyes of birds and insects do; it sees a thousand times more sharply than the human eye.
>
> **MARY MEIGS**

What is memory, and why does it change so much over time? Remember when you thought your best friend was the world's greatest? Then remember a time when she disappointed you, and suddenly you couldn't recall a nice thing she had ever done for you, only the way she hurt you? And isn't it rather surprising that this, too, passed?

We have angles of vision through which we recall our past. These angles change over time. But are we to conclude from this that our memory is not reliable? Our memory seems to be as reliable as a storage bank, but only so much can be retrieved at one time. And we retrieve according to our state of mind at the moment. The human psyche is an extraordinary construction—it opens the windows to the parts of our memory that make meaningful what we are encountering today.

One of the pleasures of midlife is that we are given a chance to see a broader spectrum all at one time.

I trust in my memory while keeping in mind the limits of its perspective.

Cheating

We must stop cheating; the whole meaning of our life is in question in the future that is waiting for us. If we do not know what we are going to be, we cannot know what we are; let us recognize ourselves in this old man or that old woman. It must be done if we are to take upon ourselves the entirety of our human state.

SIMONE DE BEAUVOIR

It does not serve us well to harbor the delusion that we will be the exception and not age to be an old woman. We cheat ourself out of our humanity. We deny ourself the vision that contains our wisdom and integrity.

Cheating is always a shortcut with ill-disguised consequences. If we pretend we know something when we do not, then how are we to be open to learning? If we copy someone else's way, then how do we ever find our own? If we handle aging by paying continual attention to our appearance, having skin tucks, seeking magic creams, and hanging out with a younger crowd, what can our deeper self do but wither?

I choose to follow the path of integrity by accepting my age.

Normalcy

So, yes, now I notice my wrinkles and beginning gray hair and have debates in my head again for the first time since I was an adolescent about what it is to be "normal."

SUSAN TURNER

We find ourselves in midlife with feelings that remind us of the awkward age of adolescence. Remember then the great mystery of "just who am I?" Set a bit free from our parents, whether by a later curfew or by our own rebellious departure from their ideas, we stared at ourselves, hoping to recognize that girl—the sprouting of new, crooked hairs in her arm pits, the swell of her emerging breasts, the desire for total immersion in the circle of her friends.

In midlife we find ourselves staring again at body changes—wrinkles, graying hair, a new handle that wants to bulge around our middle. Our loss of balance can be as great as the one we encountered at adolescence. It is again that refrain: Just who am I? We seek answers from the outside when we feel fragmented inside, for something to guide us. But we must remember the answers lie within us. For we are reconstituting even as we question and sift through our values. We are in yet another birth canal, and soon to be delivered is our midage self.

I am undergoing the normal recycling of a woman coming of age in midlfe.

Never Too Late

It is never too late to be
what you might have been.

GEORGE ELIOT

If we take inventory now of what we might have been, what do we come up with? What is stopping us from the pursuit of this now? For herein lies our work.

Mary Ann Evans, one of the greatest novelists of all time, took the name George Eliot and wrote her first novel at age forty, and thereafter she became a prolific novelist. Many women have been late bloomers, skirting around their talents, unable to come into their full power until midlife.

The woman who causes us sadness is not the one who blooms late but the one who goes to the grave with what she might have been. We do not have to be her. We can face whatever forces hold us back right now and begin to move along.

When I hear myself saying, "If only this, if only that, I might have been," I stop listening to that voice and direct myself to take an action toward my desire.

Stasis

> Life is a process of becoming, a combination of states we have to go through. Where people fail is that they wish to elect a state and remain in it. This is a kind of death.
>
> **ANAÏS NIN**

How many of us are ready and eager to move on to the next step? Perhaps we were as children when our whole life lay before us. We wanted the freedom of walking, then running. When we were in the third grade, we were eager to become fourth graders. When we were in junior high, we thought the greatest thing was high school. But as we've grown older, we've come to know the part of us that would prefer to remain behind.

Particularly in our youth-oriented culture, we are seduced into believing we had best try to stay "young" as long as we can. We cling tightly to our youthful aspects. We may associate ourselves through friendships and romantic relationships with people who are younger than us. We may spend a lot of our time struggling to create the appearance of being younger than we are. But eventually we are faced with the deadening feeling that we are not being true to ourselves. We are trying to hold onto an old self, and in so doing, we fail to give the new self adequate space to emerge.

I let go of the life stages I pass through like letting go of the changing seasons.

Changes

I have come to believe that what really happens in midlife is the need to make many radical changes as we search for a deeper understanding and expression of ourselves. Sometimes I have felt that I didn't know myself—that I had been reborn a different person. At other times, I have felt my mind and body joined in a new way and I've become more whole.

MATILE ROTHSCHILD

When our mothers were undergoing menopause, the terms most often used were "The Change" or "Change of Life." While this certainly signified a substantial change of some sort, it didn't tell us we might need to take an active part in the changing. Rather, we had the impression we would be at the mercy of our bodies.

Certainly this change does begin and end within our bodies, but as we speak of it, we discover there are other levels to our change. And at every level we can directly participate in what is happening. Some of our changes may require greater introspection. We may find ourselves on a quest to understand our spirituality. Or we may need to find a guide, such as a counselor or therapist, to point us to our feelings so that we can integrate them into all parts of our lives.

I am not a boat being tossed about in high seas.
I take an active role in my midlife and
menopausal changes.

Ageism

Ageism is a final frontier, the last metaphorical girdle from which women must free themselves.

CATHLEEN ROUNTREE

When we took on sexism, we had to take on various fronts at once. We confronted and stood eye to eye with men who were making us appear smaller and less significant than we were. But we also had to talk among ourselves to share how we really felt about who we were and who we might become. By first talking with each other, we began to step outside of this sexist belief system and to visualize and establish a belief system of our own.

Ageism, too, is endemic to our culture, and attitudes have been internalized within each one of us. As we encounter this "final frontier," we can take courage from our experience with sexism. By trusting other middle-aged and older women, we can discuss the beliefs we hold that hurt us. We can form alliances that will help us to let them go and allow a freer, older woman to emerge.

I release those attitudes that are oppressive to my growth and full expression.

Attention

It has been said the greatest gift we can give one another is rapt attention; additionally living life fully attentive to the breezes, the colors, the sorrows, and the thrills as well, is the most prayerful response any of us can make in this life. Nothing more is asked of us. Nothing less is expected.

ANONYMOUS

If we have reached midlife without learning to treasure being fully in the present, attentive to the offerings of each day, or if we have learned this lesson but forgotten it, then our work is clearly before us. This simple orientation, more than any single event or high point that we might wait for endlessly, gives us a gratifying life now, not later.

What is love if not rapt attention to another and to ourselves? Opportunities abound that we miss if our attention is scattered and not centered, if we fail to listen fully. Listening skills do not come easily. We must concentrate on focusing ourselves and learn to call ourselves back when we discover we have spaced out. But with gentle discipline, the practice of giving rapt attention will give us the gift of closer relationships.

Today, I place my full attention on whatever lies before me.

Cultivation

I do not want to die until I have faithfully made the most of my talent and cultivated the seed that was placed in me until the last small twig has grown.

KÄTHE KOLLWITZ

We each have particular talents and various opportunities to cultivate them. We often feel jealous or envious of others because they seem to have greater opportunities than we have. Perhaps they were born into a family of influence, or they had money with which to buy what they needed. Perhaps they had great confidence, instilled by supportive parents.

There is really little point in comparing ourselves to others. We all cultivate ourselves within some sort of confines, visible or invisible. The real desire to develop what we have been given comes from deep inside us, and satisfaction lies in our faithful attention to our talents and our growth. If we listen to our higher self, we seem to know the next step for our cultivation. Like a garden well-tilled, well-fertilized, and well-watered, our yield grows greater with each passing year and with each contribution we make to the development of our talents.

I attend to the next step needed for the cultivation of my unique talents and skills.

Ripening

It is sad to grow old but
nice to ripen.

BRIGITTE BARDOT

This seems to be one of the most tantalizing paradoxes of life: We must grow old in order to ripen. And this is always saddening, for after ripening comes death. What effect does this awareness have on us? Does it frighten us? Or does it heighten our sense of wanting to do the right thing for ourselves now?

By midlife most of us are content in at least some areas of our lives. Perhaps our career success is a prominent satisfaction. Perhaps we have made a nice home that represents us well. Perhaps we are happy with the way our children are developing. This is all part of our ripening. But many of us, too, realize there are areas in which we still feel stunted. Certain aspects of us have been left behind and still feel immature. These are the aspects that we want to focus our attention on now and allow to ripen. These are the areas that will only sadden us further if we do not turn to face them.

*I look to the aspects of me that have not been
allowed to ripen.*

Excitement

Change excites me. I am
fifty years old. It's when
the mind catches up with
the body.

RAQUEL WELCH

A condition such as change, inevitable
as it is, can be either exciting or deadening, leaving us flat if we try to avoid it.
At fifty it is hard not to notice we have
arrived at some milestone. But are we
catching the excitement this arrival may be heralding?

For some of us the mind is just catching up with the
body. For others the body is slowing down as we seek a lost
spiritual connection, which now seems necessary for a meaningful existence. Wherever we are in this galaxy of movement
over time, we are aware of deep changes in our foundation.
Most of us know the impulse to try to hold tight to old ways.
But we know, too, the pleasure of letting them go.

Let us entertain the excitement that comes of diving into
the river of change and embolden ourselves by remembering
the rewards of past experiences in which we have released
ourselves to float with change.

*I allow my mind and body to come together in an
empowering harmony.*

Control Over One's Body

> We need to imagine a world in which every woman is the presiding genius of her own body. In such a world women will truly create new life, bringing forth not only children, if and as we choose, but the visions and the thinking necessary to sustain, console and alter human existence, a new relationship to the universe.
>
> **ADRIENNE RICH**

Many of us have suffered in our lives over the loss of control over our bodies. As many as one-third of us have been sexually abused as children; many more of us have been raped. All of us have been forced to witness abuses of other women, without having the power to stop these abuses. We have been told what to think of our bodies, and often we have been told how to use them— have babies at this age but not at that age, be a whore, be a virgin. We need to become the presiding genius over our bodies, no matter what our age.

Especially as we enter menopause, we are presented with the choice to see things through our own eyes or see things through the eyes of others. Let us preside and make the changes that our deepest core self hungers for. She is the one, above all others, to please now.

Today, I take control of my own body and let my own genius guide her toward satisfying her needs.

Receiving

The fear of receiving resonates in the deepest levels of the psyche. To receive is to allow life to happen, to open oneself to love and delight, grief and loss.

MARION WOODMAN

For those who have spent many years in the active giving of mothering, sitting back and receiving any sort of nourishment from the universe may at first feel awkward—selfish or vacuous, as if nothing is happening. But once the channels are opened, we may feel so hungry we want everything immediately. *More, more, more.* We may need to listen more carefully to hear what our desire truly wants.

When we let receiving happen, we experience the spontaneity that makes life worthwhile. At least momentarily, we abandon collective notions of how, when, and what we should be doing and allow the emergence of our unique nature. By escaping the confines of our own rigid guidelines and expectations, we discover the tender and unknown places that have been guarded in ourselves. And we also discover new forms of expression.

I receive the energy that is coming my way today.

Growing Beyond Our Mothers

I do not want to enter middle or old age as a youngster.

DOROTHY

Some of us have mothers who were never able to grow up. Unable to fulfill themselves in reality, they sought to live out fantasy lives in which they were carried away into ecstasy. Perhaps they became voracious readers of romance novels. Perhaps they made a hobby of dressing up elegant dolls to act out the adventure they were not having themselves. They were not being in the now and being present in their bodies.

We must try to be *our* age rather than some imaginary age when we are still innocent enough to be swept off our feet and carried away. To truly be our age we may need to make a clear emotional separation from our mothers. Aspects of this may be painful, such as the feeling of leaving our mothers behind and growing beyond where they were able to grow. But ultimately we are well rewarded for our pain—because we will not be denied the richness of our age.

I take the steps necessary to grow into my age and to allow myself to enjoy it.

Surrender

At fifteen life had taught me undeniably that surrender, in its place, was as honorable as resistance, especially if one had no choice.

MAYA ANGELOU

There are many times when we have no choice. One of the most obvious and pervasive examples of this is our inability to stop the march of time. Our inevitable aging gives us a daily opportunity to practice surrender.

The challenge of surrender is brought more greatly into our awareness by menopause. Now we must surrender both to passing through a time that will not let us forget our age and to our hot flashes, emotional upheavals, and other menopausal expressions.

Surrender releases our burden and puts us in the arms of Mother Nature. It allows us to conserve and direct our energy toward the things we can change. It brings us the humility of knowing we are humans with human limitations and, in so doing, removes us from standing in our own light so that we can see the light of greater sources, whether these sources be the sun or the luminous presence in others.

I find grace in surrendering to the passage of time.

Hollywood

Going to Hollywood to talk about menopause is a little bit like going to Las Vegas to sell savings accounts.

GAIL SHEEHY

One might just as well save one's voice rather than try to convince the addict that another, more balanced way exists. A closed mind is in the nature of addiction, as is the desire for more, better, greater, grander—but not different. A more likely way to change the images of middle-aged and older women coming out of Hollywood is by our living examples. As we learn to accord greater respect to maturity, as we demonstrate how highly we prize the wisdom of our years, others will be drawn to want to reflect this.

Hollywood's one-sided portrayal of older women may sometimes infuriate us—women madly grasping backward toward youth by trying to attract younger men, the aging actresses whose faces have been pulled so tight with skin tucks they appear almost like overripe tomatoes about to explode. But let us be mindful of the superficiality of this construction. Let us not allow it to distract us from the more profound experiences we are encountering in our aging.

I recognize and take strength from the images that truly mirror me.

Experience

Experience: A comb life
gives you after you lose
your hair.

JUDITH STERN

Is this quote an April Fool's Day joke? Only insofar as the paradoxes of life provide the fodder for much of our humor.

As we gain in experience, we fear we are losing the very time we need in which to use it. We feel as if we must speed up to put our knowledge to good use or we will not get *enough* before we die. This is an illusion. We are full with our experience, and yet we often still apply it using the values of youth.

If we believe that as our experience grows every other aspect of us is shrinking, we are only setting ourselves up to react as if deprivation is the rule of the day. In fact our experience directs our growth in many areas. We may be able to truly love now as we never have before. Our creativity may be flourishing; so may our compassion and our ability to see the troubles of others. If we stop trying to quantify time and appreciate each day's moments of quality, we will find ourselves deeply full and grateful.

My experience expands me in every direction I turn.

Becoming Ourselves

I seem to have less bravado and more feeling of real stature and accomplishment.

ANONYMOUS

One of the greatest gifts of aging is the deliverance from bravado and other forms of posturing. Didn't we always use them to create a front, afraid that we didn't have enough substance, afraid to let ourselves show, plain and simple?

But now we can show ourselves. We can let our history add up. We can let our experiences enrich us. Our living takes on a greater ease because it is okay just to be who we are, to say what we want and need, and to go about seeking enjoyment in each day. We worry much less about how others perceive us. And because we are less concerned with this, we do not need to manipulate perceptions. We can let cards fall as they may and follow the path we see before us.

Today, I feel robust with my stature.

Mindstates

If at the end of life one could recall the nature of all the thoughts and emotions that had occupied the mind from moment to moment and sort them into three piles—the loving, harmonious mindstates; the neutral mindstates; and the fearful, negative mindstates—that last pile most often would tower over the others.

CHARLENE SPRETNAK

To think about our lives like this, stacked into piles according to our mindstates, encourages us to choose a positive attitude over a negative one. This is not a choice we make at the beginning of the month and adhere to rigidly until the end of the month. Rather it is a choice we make at the beginning of every day and then again moment to moment throughout the day.

Why do we so often hold ourselves in negative mindstates? Are we expressing fear? Are we supporting a wall to avoid seeing the next layer of ourselves, which we need to peel off to come closer to our core? Are we caught in a resentment that we think will prove us "right" if only we adhere to it like glue? When we make the choice to let go of our negative mindstate, its source becomes clear.

I choose today to let go of my negative mindstate and see what lies beneath it.

Second Half of Life

I believe the second half of one's life is meant to be better than the first half. The first half is finding out how you do it. And the second half is enjoying it.

FRANCES LEAR

Rarely do we hear someone say that they would prefer to go back to an earlier age, at least not unless they could take back with them what they've learned since. Isn't this evidence that the second half of life is meant to be better than the first?

By the time we get to the second half have we learned to let ourselves receive the good things? Some of us have to consciously practice allowing pleasures and rewards in our lives.

How can we attend to our wishes and desires? What are they? How can we satisfy them? Often we find ourselves caught up in old priorities that do not allow us to pursue the activities we would enjoy. Now is a good time to rearrange our priorities so that we give generously to ourselves.

I enjoy the rewards of experience that come to me in the second half of life.

Exploration

My favorite thing is to go where I've never been.

DIANE ARBUS

Which stories about explorers held you enthralled in childhood? A journey to the Antarctic? Amelia Earhart's bold piloting ventures? Edmund Hillary scaling Mount Everest? We all had a lively relationship to adventure and exploration as youngsters. Some of us have retained a better relationship to the thrill of exploration, but we each can go back to locate the explorer in ourselves.

We can approach midlife and menopause as commonplace events to drudge our way through, or we can approach them as explorers. For surely midlife is going to bring us to places where we have never been before. With a more adventurous attitude we meet ourselves with delight rather than feeling ourselves to be the victim of our changes.

I tap my exploratory nature to spirit me through my changes.

Repression

> I think if women could indulge more freely in vituperation, they would enjoy ten times the health they do. It seems to me they are suffering from repression.
>
> **ELIZABETH CADY STANTON**

We are still shedding society's expectation that women should hold back from expressing themselves sharply when they are crossed and angry. We have learned to hold anger in, turning it upon ourselves with criticism or a negative self-image. When we do this our anger is misdirected and can have the power to compromise our health.

In menopause we undergo a transition of containment in which our blood no longer gets expressed from our bodies but remains within us. Let us use this as an opportunity to be sure that our anger does not remain within us but finds healthy, direct avenues of expression.

I find a clear channel through which to express my vitality and my anger.

Setting the Record Straight

I'll be eighty this month. Age, if nothing else, entitles me to set the record straight before I dissolve. I've given my memoirs far more thought than any of my marriages. You can't divorce a book.

GLORIA SWANSON

Don't we all have the impulse from time to time to set the record straight before we die by putting down our story, if not in writing then by a full telling to someone? Perhaps we feel we have been judged by others who've not truly known what was going on with us, since no other human being can really know. Perhaps the even greater reason we want to tell our story is because we want to make the connections that will reveal our lives to *us* with greater meaning.

Awareness that we are nearing the end of our lives leads us to want to leave a legacy of the truth. We no longer want to disguise anything. If we have kept secrets, they become burdens; they have not been able to keep us alive. Quite the contrary, they have deadened us in the places where we have stayed behind a closet door. We want to come into ourselves. We want to be revealed.

I act freely to set the record straight when the desire arises.

Transformation

I don't want to get around it. I want to live it. I don't want to "treat" it or "cure" it, though I do want to honor it with curiosity and with therapy (*therapeia*), attention of the kind one devotes to sacred mysteries. I want menopause to be a soul event, which means letting it be transformative.

CHRISTINE DOWNING

The difficulty in allowing menopause to be transforming is that we are so filled with negative images of it. We fear that giving attention to our aging will set it free to happen, as if our resistance, our neglect, our turning away from it, will hold it off. And yet we are attracted to a statement such as Christine Downing's, "I want menopause to be a soul event. . . ."

Deep down we know it is. We know there is a river inside us whose mainstream is branching off from our past. To experience our soul we must go with it and not be reluctant to be our age and be in our time in history. We remember our mothers speaking of menopause in low voices. We no longer need to carry the dread this communicated to us. Respectfully, we leave our mothers' time behind and take up our own with gratitude.

I enter my menopause with my whole being.

Joy

> Menopause is the invisible experience. People don't want to hear about it. But this is the time when everything comes good for you—your humor, your style, your bad temper.
>
> **GERMAINE GREER**

The ability to reside more deeply in our bodies than we ever have before provides the foundation for revealing our humor, our style, and even our bad temper without making a show of it. For we are being ourselves without strain or effort. Our creative fountain is overflowing, too. Despite mood swings and bouts of fatigue, our energy for the things we truly want to do is abundant.

The veil of negativity that holds us apart from our age is made up of images and attitudes about women in midlife that do not originate from women in midlife. The truth is we are coming into our own, and how can this be anything other than a joyous event? Let us allow our joy to rise to the surface. Let us celebrate this new spring, even as old aspects of us are dying away.

Today, I appreciate with joy my new strengths and pleasures.

Hope

Humor is one way to acknowledge and transcend our limitations, hope is another.

KATHLEEN FISCHER

If midlife is a time of being faced more squarely with our limitations, then it is also a time of learning to transcend them. And since it is this quality—the ability to transcend—that makes aging an expansion for us, a blooming, rather than a contraction, let us pay close attention to the ways we can transcend.

Where does hope come from? Sometimes from other beings and our connection to them, sometimes from a higher force that we perceive working through us. When we despair over limitations, such as our inability to stop time from marching on, we see only the powerlessness of not being in charge. We fail to see that we are in the arms of a greater power that is providing for us.

Hope is the feeling of lightness in our hearts. With it we transcend despair. We begin to fill with hope whenever we are willing to receive it.

Hope gives me the buoyancy to transcend my limitations.

Occupancy

> Hold thought steadfastly to the enduring, the good, and the true, and you will bring these into your experience, proportionately to their occupancy of your thought.
>
> **MRS. E.**

Who occupies your house? Are you renting an apartment to despair? To your mother's critical view of you? To the one who cries "poor me"? To the expectation that "it's bound to go rotten"? We all encounter difficulties in life. That part is inevitable. But how we respond to the difficulties as well as to the joyous gifts depends on our attitude.

We adopt an attitude of holding to "the enduring, the good, and the true" by honoring long-lasting values rather than jumping at any change that offers immediate gratification. As soon as we do, we notice how many positive things come our way. We attract people who want to be there for us and to help us. When we stand up for ourselves, we discover that others are willing to stand up for us, too. Our moments of discouragement come and go, but we do not go down with them. We hold steadfast to our values and let our disappointments pass through.

I kick out any hassling tenants and rent my space to positive attitudes.

Life's Processes

When we reach this significant passage in our lives, we recognize the inexorable insistence of life's processes which pays no attention to our illusions, and does not wait for our permission. In this way menopause is like death. We all know on some level of consciousness that we are mortal, that we will die some day, but the knowledge feels unreal most of the time for most of us.

CONNIE BATTEN

Most of us feel unreal when the first signs of menopause arrive, even though we are the right age for this to happen. Somehow we thought we might be the exception. In a group meeting one of our lesbian members remarked: "I swear to you, I put this possibility out of my mind years ago and convinced myself that only heterosexual women undergo menopause." As we know, all women who reach midlife undergo menopause. There is no way to avoid it.

Our awareness of our mortality must be packed in the same suitcase of denial. We know of its inevitability, and yet we hold this knowledge apart from us. We rarely want to think or talk about the fact that we will die. For to think and talk about it brings it closer to us, and most of us are afraid of that. But, in fact, to bring it closer brings us more fully into ourselves. And here, in our core, we find the strength and the resources to accept the journey through our passages.

My life is a passage. I catch up with where I am in it today.

Confidence

I've always been a very confident person, and I just find myself growing more confident as I get older. This includes the confidence both to question and doubt myself without panicking about it. I feel that the more mature I become and the more experiences I have, the less insecure I feel about questioning.

CHARLAYNE HUNTER-GAULT

One of the greatest benefits of our aging is a deepening confidence. While we may have felt a need to prove ourselves before, now we know more about who we are and how valuable we are. Our mission is not to prove anything but to allow ourselves the space for a fruitful existence.

Questioning ourselves is essential to discovering the new territory we are exploring. Our bodies show us change is inevitable by changing on us, regardless of our wishes. They seem to be telling us it's time to check in with ourselves and make whatever re-arrangements are necessary for a new and better balance. Perhaps we want to speak out more. Perhaps we want to scale back some demanding activity, such as the painting of our home. We can make adjustments with confidence, using our accumulated wisdom.

I appreciate the steadiness of my confidence as a boon of growing older.

Descent

The death phase of our journey is a time when we feel lifeless and powerless. When we relinquish the comfort and safety of our castle walls, we abandon many of the resources that gave us the courage to go on. We are left with nothing to help us but a tiny, weak, and faltering voice. . . . This is the voice of the Self, the inner manifestation of God.

JEAN BENEDICT RAFFA, ED.D.

In midlife many of us find ourselves spiraling downward to a place of great darkness, as if the light that is guiding our journey has been lost. We have let go of some of our old ways that were no longer working for us. We feel as if we have taken off our clothes and have none to replace them. In our vulnerability we experience powerlessness over many things. We experience grief over our losses and over the areas of our lives that still feel unlived.

In our darkest hour our wisdom is forming. Like soup simmering in a cauldron, our ingredients combine and simmer to prepare us for a full-bodied emergence. We must listen to that small and faltering voice we hardly recognize, that voice of our Self. For she holds the key to the door through which we ascend back into light.

Even in my darkest descent, I trust myself and drop my defenses so that I may be reformed for a new emergence.

The Crone

I look forward to the crone. I think that's the great gift that is the balancing force for all the things we give up by aging. What we get in return is the Wise Woman. I'm looking forward to her.

ELLEN BURSTYN

The Crone is our reward for relinquishing innocence and youth. Our society tells us that we will be more valued as women if we focus our attention on retaining our youthfulness—have a face lift, buy skin creams, stay in tune with the youth culture. We must tell ourselves and reinforce to our peers that there is another way to go—toward the Wise Woman.

Our Wise Woman is the sum of all the experience we have gained with our years. She integrates it to make it useful both for our deeper understanding of the nature of life and so that we may offer counsel to others and work toward the protection of the planet. The Wise Woman holds the collective experience of the ages within her. She guides us to a fruitful existence and shows us where we can best serve.

I journey toward the Wise Woman, eager for my wisdom.

Learning

Human life is very big. There is no short cut from Minneapolis to New Mexico. . . . We learn with every cell and with time, care, pain, and love. . . . We must all go down that highway. Our life is the path of learning, to wake up before we die.

NATALIE GOLDBERG

How often do we think that surely we will reach an age where shortcuts will appear? That we have done our homework with the past and now life will become easy? But we are still on the long road, learning "with every cell and with time, care, pain, and love," ever awakening to greater awareness—an awareness that only serves to show us the places where we are still asleep.

The road, the journey, is all. Our vitality does not reside at the destination but along the way. No one thing is going to come into our lives and give us a final feeling of satisfaction. Rather, each day we are given new opportunities to be present in the now, to touch and be touched by the people we encounter, to learn the lessons that are before us. All we need to learn is humility and willingness.

Today, I stop thinking about the destination and instead see what is on the road before me.

Confirmation of Intuition

One of the fine feelings in the world is to have a long-held theory confirmed. It adds a smug glow to life in general.

M.F.K. FISHER

When we keep faith with a way of being that feels true to us, sometimes we have to sustain ourselves as we watch others take what appears to be an easier path and reach what seems to be our goal ahead of us. We are tantalized by the possibility of cutting corners and tempted to abandon our theory. But we have learned the great value of standing by our intuition and the knowledge we have gained through experience. And when eventually we are met by some confirmation in the outer world, we are rewarded by the deep feeling of well-being.

Our goal is not so much to get from point A to point B as it is to live mindfully along the way, to maintain humility and a willingness to learn, and to treat both others and ourselves with respect. If we hold to our principles and trust our way, we will often encounter that moving glow that confirms us.

Today, I trust and follow the way of meaning I have learned for myself.

Nature as Guide

If old people are lonely and say everyone has left them and no one comes to see them, I say let them go. You do not have to have other people. You have the earth, the sun, the sky, the grass. . . . Watch the grass, and you will learn how it grows from the earth and will be in touch again with the spirit that guides us.

MARTHA ST. JOHN

Sometimes we forget that human beings are but one of the many species with which we coexist. Often it is crucial for us to be connected with other human beings. But there are also times when we need to be, or find ourselves, apart from them. It is at these times that we most appreciate the guiding spirit of Nature.

Especially in spring in northern climates the miracle of grass enthralls us. We have grown accustomed to seeing the brown earth in winter. Suddenly, following a couple of days of rain, a green carpet sprouts before our very eyes, dazzling us with its color. If we have little faith in the likelihood of renewal, the grass defies our negativity.

In my midlife, I benefit from staying close to the instructions of Nature and how she unfolds her cycles.

Compulsions

> Compulsions narrow life down until there is no living—existence perhaps, but no living.
>
> **MARION WOODMAN**

The greater our disillusionment and terror, the finer an appearance we may need to make as a person with a successful life. We exert great willpower trying to cover the black hole we fear in our inner being. We dare not come home at night and relax into our being, so we drive on and on, busying the successful persona right up until we can collapse in bed. Or we stuff ourselves compulsively or drink ourselves into oblivion.

Midlife presents us with some signs of flagging energy, hinting that we cannot keep running around this same track forever without the great misfortune of having failed to live our lives. Our compulsions no longer serve us. It is time to seek whatever help we need to let them go. It is time to find communion with our being, even if that means walking through our terror.

My compulsions are no longer friends. I release them.

Idealism

Idealists . . . foolish
enough to throw
caution to the wind . . .
have advanced mankind
and have enriched the
world.

EMMA GOLDMAN

Do we think we have to give up our idealism by midlife in order to release our
grip on innocence? Or have we become
jaded by experiences in which we did
not get what we thought we wanted.
Our innocence can go without the loss
of our idealism, as long as we can distinguish between them.

Our idealism gives us vision. It enables us to see the
world as we would like it to be. And through that envision-
ing, we advance in the right direction. However, it is innocent to believe we can therefore move directly to realizing our
vision, and this will surely be corrected by our experience
with reality. But this need not discourage us. Life always presents obstacles that test our commitment.

Let us form an idealistic view of what midlife and older
ages can offer us, and let us pursue this view despite whatever
mountains we may need to scale.

*Idealism is not only for the young. I maintain mine
avidly.*

One-sidedness

Ignored organs of the psyche behave in the same way as ignored organs of the body—if you eat irregularly, your stomach is upset. Our physical organs need a certain amount of attention; we cannot afford to ignore their needs by one-sidedness. And the same is true of the organs of the psyche.

MARIE-LOUISE VON FRANZ

In midlife, any part of us we have ignored through one-sidedness seems to wail out louder than ever, "Look at me. I need your attention." Though this may disrupt other aspects of ourselves, it is an important impulse toward balance. We may be working too hard and leaving no time for our feelings to come through. We may be exercising our bodies but forgetting about our spirits.

Often when we get going, building a head of steam with our one-sided concentration on a particular effort, we can only be stopped and realigned by illness or an injurious accident. Flat on our backs, what seemed of the utmost importance before suddenly looses its oomph. We cancel plans without the imagined drastic consequences. Others step in to fill the void created by our absence. Life goes on, and into us trickles the desire to pay attention to those places we have been ignoring.

Today, I can correct my one-sidedness by awareness.

Apprehension

The apprehension of this natural period in your life will most likely outweigh any real discomfort you will actually experience. So the tremendous fear and anxiety are unnecessary. The road to overcoming these fears and anxieties is to understand fully what menopause signifies.

CAROL LANDAU, PH.D.
MICHELE G. CYR, M.D.
ANNE W. MOULTON, M.D.

If we start skipping periods and then flooding at forty-eight, we jump to the conclusion that we had better fasten our seat belts—this is only going to get worse before it gets better. If we have never had a hot flash, we may envision one as some staggering event.

One day we are sitting in a restaurant and suddenly it feels as if the restaurant is overheated. We take off a layer of clothing. We fan our face with the menu. We are about to ask the management to turn the heat down when we realize our companion appears comfortable in a sweater. We fan for another minute while we go on talking to her. Now we realize the air has become cooler again. Did someone open a window? No. We just had our first hot flash. We are both surprised and relieved—surprised that it lacked some of the drama we had been building up for and relieved that we can drop that apprehension and get on with life.

I let go of fear and anxiety and walk through menopause as it presents itself to me.

Longevity

Even the conservative American Medical Association's Council on Medical Services boldly asserts that with intelligent living we could all live to be 90 or 100 years old. This means that, before too many more decades have passed, the average woman may be living as many years after menopause as she lived before it.

LINDA OJEDA, PH.D.

How foolish and disastrous to our well-being it would be to think of ourselves as *has-beens* beginning a state of decay just because we have entered into or completed menopause. Even if we do not live into our nineties, we are probably only halfway through our adult lifetime. This is no time to begin closing up shop. It is a time to think of ourselves in our prime.

Let us relax with the idea that we have plenty of time ahead of us. We don't know when we will die, so we might as well anticipate a long life and think about what we would like to be doing in it. We have time to change. We have time to pursue interests that have remained dormant until now. Let us imagine ourselves standing before an open field, which represents the freedom of time.

I take my time as I enter into the second half of my life.

Education

> We have lived through the era when happiness was a warm puppy, and the era when happiness was a dry martini, and now we have come to the era when happiness is "knowing what your uterus looks like."
>
> **NORA EPHRON**

The knowledge about our world has changed dramatically in the past few decades. So has its availability. Most of us in midlife today know much more about our bodies than our parents and grandparents did. We know what can go wrong with them and the requirements of keeping them healthy. We are constantly challenged to learn more and become better caretakers.

Our mothers and grandmothers frequently remained in the dark about their bodies, especially their "female" organs, which were associated with sex and not spoken about freely. We have the opportunity today to have a fuller picture of our bodies. We can examine ourselves externally and internally without any sense of perversion. We can offer our observations to our doctors without embarrassment. We have both the responsibility and the power of knowing more about our bodies.

I study and equip myself with knowledge about my body.

Change

Life is change. To resist change is to work against the flow of life rather than surrender to and face it. The essence of life is the journey—the events, conditions, experiences that mold and shape us and at times knock us about.

SUSAN L. TAYLOR

If change is natural, then why do so many of us so often resist it? Do we want stasis because we think it feels good, even though, in actuality, it does not? There may be a few pleasurable moments of *I've finally got this down and now I'm all secure and cozy,* but almost immediately after that we feel some impulse to move along, because we want to seize life. We sense it passing by. We sense the deadness of trying to stay still while our world is ever turning on its axis.

To surrender to and face change we must put aside the notion that our sense of security comes from keeping things the same. We must look to other forces for security—to faith in a greater design or to trust in our constitution, that we are made of materials that won't sink but will float us down the stream of life if we allow ourselves to enjoy the journey.

I bump along with change, giving up my desire to predict the future.

Self-definition

Most of us have foolish ideas about who we are and many, many rigid rules about how life should be lived.

LOUISE L. HAY

It's shocking when we discover in ourselves a quality we dislike that we had thought only belonged to others. And it's humbling when we realize we are living within very strict boundaries and no one is setting those boundaries but us.

In midlife we have both the urge and the opportunity for breaking out of any prisons we have placed around ourselves. For example, if we think that it is sinful to sleep more than eight hours, let us give in and see what happens. Maybe we will discover a vivid dream life in the ninth hour. If we have pouted for years because our spouse doesn't like to travel in the way we yearn to, who says we cannot travel alone? Perhaps this is exactly what we are meant to do.

What is our idea of who we are? Let us be grateful for the knowledge we have of ourselves, but this shouldn't obscure the parts that remain hidden. Let us open ourselves to further knowledge of ourselves.

I appreciate the humility that comes of realizing how much and yet how little I know of myself.

Isolation

Isolated from other women and with less than ten years of schooling in the rural Midwest, my mother believed that menopause could ruin a woman's life. Indeed, when a neighbor gradually sickened and died, my mother attributed her death to the fact that the woman "just never recovered from her change of life."

JUDY GRAHN

Many of our mothers encountered the same fears we are going through now, only they festered with worry without being able to compare notes with their neighbors. Having worried ourselves as children or adolescents about what was happening to our mothers, is it any wonder we inherited a certain amount of anxiety about The Change?

We have the good fortune today of going through menopause at a time when taboos are being broken. We do not need to be isolated with our experience. We do not need to imagine the worst when we might instead speak with our neighbors and friends. We may find ourselves reluctant to talk, and our words may come haltingly at first, for this history of silence is deeply embedded in us, but as we share we become more emboldened as well as more knowledgeable. We are relieved not to be alone.

Keeping my fears isolated only enlarges them. Today, I will share them with someone.

Wrinkles

I enjoy my wrinkles and regard them as badges of distinction. I've worked hard for them.

MAGGIE KAHN

How did Maggie Kahn come to enjoy her wrinkles? Did she first struggle through a period of rejection as she looked in the mirror? *Oh, no, that can't be me!* Did she negotiate? *I'll attend you better, apply those skin creams more regularly.* Chances are we all go through certain steps in a process of acceptance, much like the stages associated with grief. For it is quite natural that we do grieve our lost youth.

However long these stages take, it is nice to know we are moving toward acceptance, a time when we can admire our wrinkles and see them as a reminder of our accumulated experience and wisdom. These badges of distinction become us and show us to be the finely seasoned beings we are.

I study my face in the mirror today and notice with pride how my wrinkles reveal me.

Aging

It is quite wrong to think of old age as a downward slope. On the contrary, one climbs higher and higher with advancing years, and that, too, with surprising strides. Brain-work comes as easily to the old as physical exertion to the child. One is moving, it is true, toward the end of life, but that end is now a goal, and not a reef in which the vessel may be dashed.

GEORGE SAND

The older one becomes, the less one thinks of death as a tragedy and the more it becomes the meaningful ending. We often hear old people express this feeling: "I've lived long enough. I hope the end comes soon now." Sometimes, even then, we deny the sincerity of their expression and try to convince them to reorient themselves toward a future. "Don't think like that," we tell them. "You've got plenty of life left in you."

What if we are to think of life as one long climb, accelerating first in one aspect, then in another? We see then that we are provided with natural compensations. As our physical strength and stamina declines, our mental powers may be rising, as may our spiritual powers and our ability to sit still longer to receive them.

Nature has provided me with undeniable life cycles. My job is to accept them.

Spring

Spring
the invitation
All who care to
    participate
frivolous
or feverish
may apply

MAUREEN BRADY

How does spring instruct us about midlife? It shows us the renewal that comes after the dormancy of the inward season. We can think of our menopause as an inward season, one in which we learn to contain ourselves after our growth through youth and young adulthood. Sporadically, perhaps gradually, our blood ceases flowing. All through this process we are mindful of the fact that we will emerge at the other end, new in some way.

In spring we watch the buds swell until they burst open with new leaves and flowers. Despite the tenderness of their newness, they are resilient and march relentlessly onward to greater strength and certainty. We, too, are like this as we emerge from our menopause. Our new identity grows stronger with each passing moment. Let us appreciate the nature of our spring.

Spring is the great season of ebullience. I let its mood infect my own emergence.

Contentment

> I seem not to have grown older in the year, but more content with whatever age it is I am.... There may well be the enduring challenge of the 365 steps up the face of the Temple of the Dwarf at Chichén Itzá, but the certainty that I shall never again climb them no longer disturbs me.
>
> **DORIS GRUMBACH**

Certain years become years of reckoning and adjustment to our new age. Perhaps we have felt this at forty, forty-five, and fifty, and we will feel it again at sixty, seventy, and eighty. We face these birthdays with reluctance. We don't like being reminded of our body's limitations. Often we grow nostalgic for the good old days when we could spend an entire day working in the garden and be tired, yes, but still stand straight at the end of the day.

It is often easier to live in the past than to reckon with the present. But this does not give us the full pleasure of being alive and inside our skin today. Being in the present is often all we really need to stop being grouchy and feel whole and glorious with what we have right now.

*I patiently give myself the time to adjust, knowing
I will again reach contentment with my age.*

Estrogen

If estrogen were prescribed for men instead of women and the drug had the same history, you can be sure it would have been exposed on *60 Minutes,* discussed by the *McLaughlin Group,* debated in the House, investigated by the Senate, and settled in the courts with the usual fine, jail, and community service.

GAYLE SAND

Estrogen is one of the most-debated drugs of our time. Arguments in its favor include the prevention (or at least the slowing down) of osteoporosis, the diminution of hot flashes, and the avoidance of vaginal dryness. However, it has been linked to an increased risk of breast cancer. Its opponents also point out that when our bodies are not provided with artificial estrogen, they begin to manufacture more of it in places other than the ovaries—fat cells and the adrenal glands.

We each must come to our own decision about whether to use Estrogen Replacement Therapy according to our individual problems and the approach that suits us best. But let us take the time to understand both the benefits and the possible consequences. Let us also demand of the medical community greater attention and clarification of this important subject.

I study the literature, both traditional and alternative, and participate in a decision about estrogen that will have important consequences to my body.

Forgiveness

Forgiveness is the act of
admitting we are like
other people.

CHRISTINA BALDWIN

Midlife nudges us to accept ourselves as
human beings with our individual
foibles and limitations. If we are carrying along a train of resentments, we can
take this time to examine them, to see what they are made
of. Did we have superhuman expectations of others, which
they failed to meet? Are we defended by our righteousness,
convinced that we have never failed anyone in quite the
same way?

Forgiving ourselves and others is a humbling act, and it
happens when we have the willingness to open our hearts to
our humanity. If we simply say, "I want to forgive so and so,"
the process will be underway. Where we held hard-and-fast
feelings, we find ourselves softening. Where we thought we
were exempt, we see that we, too, may have disappointed
others, even when we never intended to. Soon we discover
that some hard-and-fast distinctions we previously held have
blurred and that we have given greater freedom as much to
ourselves as to the person we have forgiven.

*Forgiveness is always an option. Today, I take the risk
of choosing it.*

Loneliness

In the communal Cherokee culture, the worst curse one person could call down on another was not death, but loneliness. Perhaps it is the worst curse in any culture. "Alone and grieving . . . " As I travel about the country, how often I hear that feeling expressed. It is part of the modern, fragmented life.

MARILOU AWIAKTA

When we examine our fears about aging, chances are that the fear of loneliness leads the pack. Certainly in our urban industrial communities, many older people who have lost their spouses live alone. Though we know that one can also be lonely in the company of others, we project the greatest loneliness on those who are alone.

As we enter midlife and quite naturally look ahead to our older life, we can turn our fear of loneliness into an activism now and work toward creating a greater community. We can volunteer in a local project that benefits seniors. We can work for social and political changes that will result in greater security for elders. And we can attend to our own loneliness by recognizing how it comes when we hold ourselves apart.

Today, I take an active role in an act of community building.

Health

Nowadays, in our culture we call the self-healing system the immune system. . . . In India it is called *prana,* and identified with the breath of life, in Japan and China a similar concept is called *chi.* . . . Both concepts include a wider and deeper vision of the human organism than the Western concept of the immune system, but we are probably all talking about the same thing.

RIMA HANDLEY

Whether we are going to have a difficult or an easy menopause, the best way we can enter it is with our bodies in good health. A certain amount of bone loss is inevitable with the diminution of estrogen, yet if we have taken good care of ourselves by eating a healthy diet and exercising properly, we will start out with greater bone density and will also lose less along the way.

Likewise with our mental attitude. If we attend to balancing our lives and fulfilling our emotional and spiritual needs, when our hormones begin to ebb and surge we will not necessarily avoid mood swings and feelings of grief or depression but we will be able to more readily cope with these feelings. Let us think of grooming our immune system by the ways we attend to self-care in our daily lives.

I nurture my whole being as food for my immune system.

Feelings

Our feelings are our
most genuine paths to
knowledge.

AUDRE LORDE

When in doubt about which fork in the
road to take, let us follow the message
of our hearts. Sometimes this requires
sorting through mixed feelings, ferret-
ing out the causes of our fears and addressing them, and talking with others for clarification. Each of our mixed feelings is
a genuine path, there for us to follow.

Sometimes we question whether or not we have any feelings at all about a matter. Take our aging, for instance.
Perhaps we hear ourselves saying to others: "I don't have any
feelings about it one way or the other." But when we truly
examine our condition, we discover that we have shut off
from our feelings and put a mask over them. We may then act
as if we confidently, indeed arrogantly, know our direction,
when in fact the route to our heart is closed. Or we may feel
lost and imbalanced, which cautions us not to proceed without finding ourselves first.

With awareness of this condition, we can seek our feelings and always find them waiting for us.

*I trust that my feelings, openly met, will be my faithful
guides.*

Violation

Whenever the Earth and female Powers are respected, the female body, in all of its transformations, is respected.

JANE CAPUTI

Just as the female body has been violated both in exploitative imagery and in crimes such as rape, the earth is being repeatedly threatened and often mutilated.

The history of disrespect and violation of "female Powers" runs so deep we often fail to recognize its influence on us. But the more we embrace our own powers, the greater the chance of being ridiculed or punished for aligning ourselves with them. For instance, can we think of calling ourselves witches without a tremor of the terror provoked by witch burnings?

We can take back our center both by standing for our truth and our full power and by standing for the earth, respecting her wondrous being and her tremendous power. She is whole and unto her own. She is not man-made. Nor are we.

I refuse to feel violated by any images that deny me or the earth our powers.

Invisibility

We need to raise our voices a little more, even as they say to us "This is so uncharacteristic of you." Invisibility is not a natural state for anyone.

MITSUYE YAMADA

Women have long had to cope with invisibility in many realms. Our beauty has been acclaimed as have our mothering instincts, but what of the rest of us—our intelligence, our mastery of our art, our voice in politics and worldly matters? We have had to struggle to become visible in these areas. We have often had to run circles around men to achieve the same recognition.

Now we face midlife, and looking ahead to see how older women fare, we see that we will have to face the invisibility problem all over again. Let us raise our voices now to create a better climate in which to age. We need space to allow our wisdom to come to fruition. With each age we enter we need to hear ourselves describe our true experiences, and we need to be able to hear our elders describe theirs.

I sound off loud and clear and let myself be seen and heard.

Being

In the bigger scheme of things the universe is not asking us to *do* something, the universe is asking us to *be* something. And that's a whole different thing.

LUCILLE CLIFTON

"The universe is asking us to *be* something." What does this mean? It means we recognize our breath as the breath of life, a gift of every moment. It means we are one of many creatures on this planet, affecting all others and being influenced by them. It means we are responsible for fulfilling our mission in being here. It means there is love at the root of our connection to all beings. Let us open our hearts to reach out with that love and receive it.

In midlife, as in all ages, we are presented with opportunities to deepen our sense of being. This being Self is not divorced from what we know and what we do. But neither does it flourish if we allow ourselves to be categorized and defined by our knowledge and skills and the pride we take in using them. The deepening of our being comes from integrating all our parts.

Today, I honor my being.

Obsession

The trouble with the rat
race is that even if you
win, you're still a rat.

LILY TOMLIN

Often we go round and round, running
faster and harder, thinking that by
doing so we are going to get ahead or at
least catch up. We do not recognize our
one-sidedness as obsession. We think that we are getting
somewhere. We think that if we try this hard, surely we will
be rewarded with the results we desire. Especially in midlife, if
we fail to realize that some of the ways that satisfied us in the
past want to be left behind, we are prone to fall into the trap
of obsessive racing, which keeps us out of breath but gets us
nowhere.

When our frustration is great enough, we stop and entertain the notion that perhaps in stillness we can hear our soul
speak to us. We are weary of the rat race and ready to admit
we are not getting much enjoyment out of being a rat. It may
be frightening to let go of our obsessive behavior because
often it is blocking uncomfortable feelings from coming to
the surface. In our stillness, we can feel what is holding us
apart from ourselves. And underneath that, we find and take
direction from our center.

I cease racing and let new values emerge.

Hero

One must think like a
hero to behave like
a merely decent human
being.

MAY SARTON

We each have the archetype of the hero
within us, despite the fact that most
heros we have read about in literature
are male. Who is the female hero? Is she
the mother who manages to shepherd
herself and her children through the welfare system when she
has no other choice, accepting all sorts of humiliation but
showing up to stand in line regardless? Is she the woman who
stands up to her boss against unjust conditions in the work-
place? Perhaps she is the woman in you who holds certain
values dear and strives to behave according to them.

Midlife is a time that shows us the nature of change is
gradual. It grounds us to the daily rituals and feelings of living. And with this focus, we see how the heroic infuses our
vision of who we want to be and how we act, in actions seemingly small and insignificant but which add up to something
grand.

*I find the heroic gesture within me and express it
often in my ordinary life and ways of being.*

Leadership

> I suppose leadership at one time meant muscles; but today it means getting along with people.
>
> **INDIRA GANDHI**

By midlife many of us have well-developed leadership abilities. We have learned to speak our minds. We have a strong sense of our values and how we can abide them. We have a steady stance from which to act on our principles.

One senses world leadership under women like Indira Gandhi would come closer to satisfying our desire for peace on the planet. Women seem to give up muscle more easily than men and perhaps are more motivated to get along with others. How better can we put our life experience to work if not by a practice of getting along with others? This does not mean "making nice" or people pleasing. To get along with others we must bump against the parts of ourselves that are turned off, disagreeable, deprived, or upset by the ways of others. If we neither fight nor flee in response to these reactions, we deepen our discovery of ourselves in all our aspects.

I put my leadership abilities to good use in the world.

Stages of Growth

I've already spent enough of my adulthood trying to go back and capture my lost youth. I don't want to spend my old age going back for my middle age. I want to have it while it's here.

MARTA

If we see life as a natural progression of stages, the value of being present for each of them is apparent. Yet we have more demarcated rituals for coming of age from adolescence to adulthood—moving away from our parental household, graduation, marriage—than we do for our later stages of coming of age into middle-aged maturity. But it is wise to neither skip forward nor try to cling to a stage that is over. We sense that people who jump ahead, missing a period of independence before getting married, for instance, deprive themselves of experiences that there will be no making up for.

As we move into midlife, it is important to recognize we are on a cusp, closing out a period of our youth and opening more deeply to the texture and dimensions of the next phase. As women we can use our menopause as the guiding marker by which we recognize our altering status. In so doing, we bring ourselves into the rich offerings of this stage of life.

I approach each stage of life with high value. I don't want to miss anything.

Action

Our life is composed greatly from dreams, from the unconscious, and they must be brought into connection with action. They must be woven together.

ANAÏS NIN

In the reappraisal of midlife, we catch glimpses of our dreams, the ones that have been realized and the ones that have slipped by because they never became grounded with action. Our dreams often instruct us or provoke us. They awaken us to unlived desires, forewarn us when we are walking on shaky ground, even sometimes guide us to the right form of action. But we must sit up and take notice and bring the dream along, into the conscious realm, in order to be able to take action.

Any day is a good day for asking ourselves the question: In what area of my life do I not have what I want? How can I go about seeking to have it? The next step is to act. For instance, if you answered, "I do not have a friend who truly knows me as I know myself today," your action might be to take yourself out to community activities that draw people of like interests and begin to look for a new friend. Day by day, action by action, we bring our dreams down to earth until they become our reality.

I choose actions that are inspired by my dreams and see my dreams become reality.

Power of Language

Psychologies, especially feminist psychology, have revealed agencies of power to me, until it's increasingly clear how powerful language itself is as an agent of repression, dominance, and destruction, and of change itself.

JANE MILLER

Language is fluid. It has often been used to repress us—"hag," "bitch," "whore," "witch," "nag." It can also be used to break us free from old meanings and perceptions that eat away at our self-image.

Let us seize language and use it boldly to create striking models of the power of our aging. Let us speak freely and loudly of the wisdom of our elders. Let us write and speak of our mothers and grandmothers with great respect for their examples, for the sustenance they have provided, as they faced or continue to face their aging. Let us uphold and champion their dignity with the language that we use.

I manifest my own power through the power of language rather than letting others use it to victimize me through the creation of negative images of aging.

Middle Age

The signs that presage growth, so similar, it seems to me, to those in early adolescence: discontent, restlessness, doubt, despair, longing, are interpreted falsely as signs of decay. In youth one does not as often misinterpret the signs; one accepts them, quite rightly, as growing pains.

ANNE MORROW LINDBERGH

Many of us in midlife encounter blocks of restlessness and longing. We question why we are so unhappy when, indeed, many of our earlier ambitions have been satisfied. Perhaps we wanted children and we had them and have now seen them off on their own. Perhaps our career has provided us fair amounts of material success and recognition for important work accomplished. And yet we are still restless. These things do not content us. And this is probably a good thing. For would we grow any further if they did?

There is no reason to think we are too old for growing pains. We always seem to carry an illusion that life will reach a fixed point beyond which struggle will no longer be necessary. Death may be this moment, but we often expect it of each stage of maturity as well.

Longing, discontent, and often despair awaken me to further the needs and desires I am fortunate enough to have. I heed them today.

Anxiety

Anxious feeling can be in some as always an ending to them, it can be in some as always a beginning in them of living, there are some who have it in them as their own way of living.

GERTRUDE STEIN

In midlife we begin to prize every state with which we have grown familiar. Up until now we may have tried to push away our anxiety, not wanting to have it at all or at least not for very long. We have tried all sorts of tactics for avoidance to little avail. If we look at it through the expansive eye of Gertrude Stein, we see it may sometimes be serving us with a friendly purpose—bringing us to a beginning of living.

We may be anxious about our menopause, about the very notion of making a passage from which we will emerge changed. We may feel as if we finally just settled into the comfort of our adulthood, and now we are moving downstream to yet another new place. Life does not halt for us when we feel left behind. But also, anxiety, especially when unrecognized, tends to speed up our perception of time. Let us court our anxiety, listen to what it might have to say, and then console it.

My anxiety is a true feeling, trying to express something. Today, I acknowledge and respond to it.

The Unbegun

Can anything be sadder than work left unfinished? Yes; work never begun.

CHRISTINA ROSSETTI

Midlife presents us with a fertile time for a survey of both what we have left undone and what we have never begun. Perhaps we say, "Oh dread, I don't even want to think about that!" But if we can convince ourselves to take a more positive attitude, we will see that we are shunning an opportunity for further awakening. If we check in with our heart and soul, we will find our desire to respond to this opportunity.

The unbegun begins as soon as we bring the desire into our awareness. With it may come grief for its neglect in the past. Perhaps it is a talent we have never allowed a chance to blossom. Perhaps it is a new way of loving we have spent all these years preparing for. Perhaps it is a community project we have long harbored as a good idea but kept hidden away within us. Without further ado, let us simply begin it.

I begin my unbegun today.

Body Language

We have so many words for states of the mind, and so few for the states of the body.

JEANNE MOREAU

For the mind we have confused, overwhelmed, lucid, out of it, sharp, clear, concentrated. We have murky, mixed up, mindless, mired. What do we have for the states of the body? Well, ill, tired, rested. Painful, feverish, achy, jumpy. Most of our words for the states of the body apply to being sick or being well. We have relatively few words to describe the states of transition our bodies encounter as they move through stages of growth.

In adolescence we speak of raging hormones, jittery legs that can't sit still, excessive energy. Most of our descriptions are based on a comparison to a state presumed to be more normal. In menopause we do likewise. We speak of loss of hair, loss of acuteness of memory, loss of bone density, loss of sleep from night sweats. Would our attitudes be influenced by a different vocabulary? Imagine a series of words that gave the ring of reassurance that we were in the right place at the right time. Our cells are following Nature's plan for us, just as they did when we passed through adolescence.

I shamelessly search for the words that describe the experience of my being during menopause.

Perennials

In the middle of my life I am discovering the rewards of staying put in one place for a decade. My plants keep extending their underground networks and offer me expansion with each year.

JANINE

The wonder of spring brings us to a sense of renewal within. For suddenly everything is blooming. If we have planted perennials, we are duly rewarded now. What we remember once as a small potted plant has ranged out to cover half a garden. The few irises we once put in have now been divided many times and moved to many locations. Some have even been given away to others.

We, too, are perennials. We arrive each new year with our roots extended further into life's rich earth. Our underground network is ever expanding; even in dormant times, it is in preparation for expansion. The more consciously we are present in our lives today, the greater the splendor of our flowering.

Let no one convince us that coming into the second half of adulthood at fifty means it is time to be withered. Quite the contrary, for many of us full blooming has only just begun.

My midlife is a time of blossoming I do not need to deny.

Mystery

The initial mystery that attends any journey is: How did the traveller reach his starting point in the first place?

LOUISE BOGAN

Often we spend our energy trying to figure ourselves out, which is a futile job, since we are exploring in the realm of mystery. We are trying to discover knowledge that is not ours to know.

We are formed by many influences. By midlife we gain a clear picture of this. We recognize the parts of us that resemble our parents—our gestures, our attitudes, some of the qualities we liked about them and some that we didn't. We recognize our own nature and the spaciousness we've gained whenever we found ways to receive and express it. We realize that we've crossed paths with many people in our lives; a number of them have shown us new ways of being, broadening our journey.

Still we cannot know exactly what brings us to the starting point we have arrived at today. With humility, we recognize that greater universal forces are always exerting their pull on us, drawing us one way or another as if toward the pole of a magnet. Let us relax our effort to crack the mystery and become a part of it.

I question what forms me, but I do not need to answer the questions.

Romanticizing Age

I have no romantic feelings about age. Either you are interesting at any age or you are not. There is nothing particularly interesting about being old—or being young, for that matter.

KATHARINE HEPBURN

People prove interesting not because they are old, or young, or the perfect in-between age, but because they are in their lives, passionately engaged with themselves and the world around them. We are interesting when we are interested—open to knowledge, intuition, and the messages of our hearts. We are interesting when we have room for spontaneity—when our emotions flow freely and we are capable of awe and of allowing ourselves to play.

Age is often romanticized. Surely she must be special if she is ninety-nine, we think. And perhaps there is truth in this, but it's true because most people who live to one hundred have remained highly engaged with life.

At midlife the romantic notion is that we should take pride and glory from *not* looking our age. This is of little interest to those of us who are actually passing through. What makes us vital is being fully alive in our transition, not exerting energy trying to preserve a youth that is already past.

I interest myself with my current relationship to the world.

Passing One's Prime

When did I pass my prime? Yesterday? Or will it be tomorrow?

BARBARA

What does it mean to be in one's prime? It is one of those visualized heights after which we are supposed to expect decline rather than a continuing expansion. Truer to the actual experience of aging is the visualization of a series of moments, years, decades even, when life opens out in one direction or another.

As we move into midlife we may open out in the direction of our spirituality. We may find our career in full bloom. We may be in the prime of at last being comfortable in our own skin.

In our older ages we have a good chance of coming into a prime in relation to our sense of inner peace.

A prime is not something to be self-conscious about. If I am in one, I am probably too whole-heartedly involved in my life to notice it.

Inheritance

Just as you inherit your
mother's brown eyes, you
inherit a part of yourself.

ALICE WALKER

Year after year different aspects of our
inheritance come into our awareness
and lend us new perspective. Much of
life is a journey both to be loyal to our
inheritance and to see ourselves separate from it. For instance, we see our parents in our faces, in our hands, and in
our bodies. Then we also see the legacy we give ourselves to
be our own person.

As we grow older we often become more interested in our
inheritance. We may need to go back to the land of our ancestors to get a better sense of our collective inheritance. We
find, then, that some of the characteristics we once thought
were individual to our parents actually ran deep in our heritage.

A sad fact that comes with midlife is that our elders are
dying or sometimes losing the reliability of their memories.
Those people who are our source for hearing stories about the
previous generations no longer provide this commentary. We
must seek ways on our own to grasp the story of our past.

*I am supported by my inheritance and its blend of
sources.*

Living Fully

I don't want to get to the end of my life and find that I just lived the length of it. I want to have lived the width of it as well.

DIANE ACKERMAN

At any age we can fall prey to the attitude that we can't wait to finish a thing—this job, parenting a child until he or she goes off to college, the process of renovating or decorating our house, or the transition represented by menopause. We begin to focus on the notion that reaching a point of closure will complete us and make us full. When we are of this mind, we often miss the width of life all around us.

The width of life comes in partaking of the process. If we spend our workday stealing glances at the clock to see how near we are to closing time, we may well miss the smile of a coworker at noon, the challenge of a work problem that presents itself, the peace of deep concentration. So, too, in all other areas of life.

Today, I live the full breadth of my life.

Truth

Truth is the only safe
ground to stand upon.

ELIZABETH CADY
STANTON

Why should we even attempt to stand
on anything other than the safe ground
of the truth? Often we are afraid of the
truth because it is too painful; it exposes
parts of the picture we defend ourselves from by hiding. For
example, we are angry with a friend for disappointing us by
failing to show up and give support at an important time.
Rather than reveal our anger, we lie to her about why we
won't be able to attend an event of hers. Who does this lie
benefit? It may shield us from facing our own fear about our
anger, but that does not serve us nor repair our friendship.

As we grow older, we realize these lies have been detours
or stop-gap measures that have not given us ourselves. When
we have chosen to protect others rather than to reveal our
feelings, we have injured ourselves. We have made ourselves
invisible by trivializing our feelings, and then we have felt
badly about being devious. As we grow in self-respect, we see
that each situation merits the truth and that we deserve the
firm ground the truth provides.

*Today, I tell the truth and handle its consequences as
they come.*

Unity

> If the first woman God ever made was strong enough to turn the world upside down all alone, these women together ought to be able to turn it back, and get it right side up again.
>
> **SOJOURNER TRUTH**

The world as we know it in our contemporary culture is turned upside down about menopause and the aging of women. We hear notions bandied about that we are "over the hill," "past our prime," "shriveled prunes," and other descriptions that suggest we are of little consequence and certainly not a force to be reckoned with. Yet we know that we are *on a hill,* looking at a great expanse, *in our prime,* and *proudly wrinkling up with our wisdom.* Many of us have never felt stronger or smarter.

Let us not make the mistake of believing that we need to wait for physicians or politicians or psychologists or some other authorities to right the distortions in our world about aging. Surely women united have the strength to turn the world right again. We must verify what comes with this age by speaking to each other and believing each other. Let us not underestimate our power to set the record straight.

I do my research by listening to my own experience and that of other women.

Vitality

At sixty, I was hopelessly frail, yet, in some incredible way, I was more vital than ever. My physical weakness, after the heartbreaking strain of a divided life, appeared to lend light and warmth to my imagination. Pain had not defeated me. It had made me defiant and more confident of my inner powers.

ELLEN GLASGOW

Some of us have lived with physical disabilities for our whole lives. Others have only encountered physical frailty in recent years, through the aging process. We have all had pain at some time and can recognize how it brought us to our inner powers when nothing less threatening might have motivated us.

And what did we find there? The fullness of our imagination, the staying power of our heart's message that we were more than this pain, the compassion to appreciate the pain of others.

There is a vitality that comes with youth and physical vigor. There is also a vitality that comes with age.

Regardless of any physical frailty, I appreciate my vitality today.

Complaining

Complaining is one voice of the dark goddess. It is a way of expressing life, valid and deep in the feminine soul. It does not, first and foremost, seek alleviation, but simply to state the existence of things as they are felt to be to a sensitive and vulnerable being.

SYLVIA BRINTON
PERERA

It is often through complaining that we hear ourselves begin to define what needs changing in our lives. We complain about our deprivation in the emotional realm, or the economic realm, or the spiritual realm. We complain that we have been held back, that events of our past have kept us from fully participating in life. We complain that we have been hurt, that life has given us too many punches. We complain that we are bone tired. We complain that we are ill.

What is our deep complaint today? Let us truly listen to our complaints and trust them to represent some aspect of our reality. When we push them aside, they only grow louder, asserting themselves to be heard. When we hear them, we can begin to understand and respect the needs they are expressing. And then we can take actions to alleviate them.

Today, I give a hearing to my complaints.

New Space

The new space . . . has a kind of invisibility to those who have not entered it.

MARY DALY

Why do we not see the new space of our midlife before it presses down upon us? We notice the unappealing images portraying older women as frail and without power, but these do not draw our attention. So we leave blank the new space until we come right up to it and discover we are in a perimenopausal stage, then a menopausal one. Even during this time, we rarely look ahead.

Are we afraid to look forward into our aging because of the vulnerability that comes with it? Are we afraid of the shadow of death, which lies, we hope, at the far end of our aging?

We are a generation of women capable of creating bold images of a Cronedom to which all women may be drawn. Let us visualize that new space filled with confident white-haired women sharing their wit, wisdom, and compassion with one another, with the younger generations, and with the forces of power in the world.

I visualize the new space I am about to enter in the next few years.

Counsel

One acquires a sort of authority from the accumulation of experience at the same time one is pretty much written off by youth as having any value. Still I find it important to spout off generously when I have an opinion, never knowing exactly how much it will be heard.

HELEN

The naïveté of youth is so much easier to see from the vantage point of age. When our youthful relatives and friends are making impulsive choices, we watch from afar, wishing we could do their homework for them, yet knowing that no one can do that for somebody else. They must follow in our footsteps by gaining their own experience.

What we can do is share our experiences and offer our opinions. We are free from the need for their approval, and this gives us the ability to advise them selflessly, to remain unattached to their responses and the ultimate outcome of their choices. By offering our wisdom we are strengthening the chain of generations, which is meant to support young and old alike.

Today, I speak my mind lovingly to the younger generation.

Acceptance of Death

[Acceptance of my own death] means to me that I am ready to die whenever the time comes; that I'll try at least to live every day as if it were my last one, and, needless to say, hope for a thousand more days like today.

ELISABETH KÜBLER-ROSS

As we enter midlife we become more mindful of a precious commodity—time. There seems to be less of it. The years go by more rapidly, or at least so it seems. We see our death somewhere on the horizon, where we once found it nearly impossible to imagine such a limit. This gives us cause to arrange our lives to achieve what we want now.

Part of our work is to accept our death. This may mean going through the stages Elisabeth Kübler-Ross has described, which most people encounter upon being informed that they are seriously ill, including denial, anger, bargaining, and depression—all before acceptance. Throughout our aging, we may encounter these stages even when we are not seriously ill. For instance, menopause may break our denial about the fact that we are not the exception, that we, too, are aging. Or, through the deaths of our parents or close friends, we may face death and imagine what it will mean for ourselves.

With acceptance of death comes a peace that I have long sought.

Difference

We are frightened of
what makes us different.

ANNE RICE

We all know the urge to belong. When we are young it is comforting to be a part of our family, to know that we look like them and share the same blood. If we are adopted, for years we may fear our difference means we don't belong, but we come to understand that the shared history we have with our family creates an equally important bond.

In adolescence we emphasize our differences from our elders, seeking to establish an individual identity; we act fearless and flaunt our differences. Yet with our peers we usually struggle to appear the same, revealing our continuing fear of being different.

One of the pleasures of aging is to become more comfortable and accepting of our differences from others and to appreciate the enrichment we gain from the diversity of people we know. Yet even with this greater acceptance, we may discover we are fearful that our own aging will create differences between ourselves and others. If we have not accepted our changing identity, we may fear being shunned because of being older.

Today, I embrace my differences and emanate the acceptance I feel.

Generosity

One can never pay in gratitude; one can only pay "in kind" somewhere else in life.

ANNE MORROW LINDBERGH

As we grow older, generosity becomes a more ready impulse in us. We have *more,* or at least we have the feeling that we have more. Thus we have more to give. Looking back over our lives with the distance of time, we are also better able to see the many acts of generosity that have come our way from others and how these acts have given us hope and affirmation.

Giving back provides a concrete form for our gratitude. Often the giving back is not done with the same person who gave to us. We can trust that the universe contains us all, and energy given will be returned to us "in kind." For instance, if we have received the guidance of a mentor, let us mentor another; if someone once consoled us in our grief, let us console another.

Today, I take pleasure in the free flow of my generosity.

Valuing Ourselves

Women who set a low
value on themselves
make life hard for other
women.

NELLIE L. MCCLUNG

We stop and take notice when we see a woman who places a high value on herself. We appreciate her, and she becomes a role model for us, an example of the kind of energy we would like to transmit. She helps us believe that if we work through negative messages, we, too, will have and reflect high self-esteem.

What of the woman who says: "Oh menopause, do you really think it deserves all this hoopla? It was nothing to me." She may make us question if we are making too much of our feelings and our changes. But when we refuse to let her minimilizing minimilize us, when we reply that the more attention we give to this transition the more we realize how important a time it is, we discover that her interest is piqued. Perhaps she just did not know how to place a high value on it alone.

I follow the path of the woman who places high value on herself.

Rituals

We live in a culture bare of transforming rituals. Yet psychological development seems to require them.

JANE R. PRÉTAT

As we leave behind the structure and safety of our old ways and move into the new territory brought to us through our aging, many of us flounder in confusion and huddle in despair. Perhaps our confusion would be lessened if we had clear rituals to acknowledge our transition. The road we are traveling would be less vague.

Given the general absence of rituals, many of us, consciously or unconsciously, develop small rituals of our own. Perhaps we take a long-desired journey. Perhaps we make a new garden or redesign our old one to become a place that will deliver greater bounty with less labor. Perhaps we begin an investigation of our spirituality or develop a new spiritual practice. Perhaps our health requires us to closer abide by the needs of our bodies, and our ritual takes the form of meeting dietary needs, exercising, or tending to an illness.

I see how the small rituals I have adopted in my life are helping me mark a transition.

Silence

Sitting in a decent silence, enjoying the presence of the you that does not talk, and liking even better the absence of the one that does. One's mind open, in case there is any peace about; but turning away from the too personal, in search of the impersonal— we need a good deal of blankness for that.

FLORIDA SCOTT-MAXWELL

Depending upon how extroverted or introverted we are, we all require a certain amount of time for being silent. But this need seems to grow larger as we pass through midlife and move toward our older years, especially for those of us who have discovered the wealth of our inner lives.

In times of transition, we only delay the process if we fail to get quiet and allow changes to gestate. Suppose we are overly engaged with our position as an executive, yet we really want to direct theater before our best years have passed us by. We noisily clamor about with our old ways, grumbling but barely giving ourselves a moment to examine our quandary. Our old ways become awkward; we stumble as we drag them behind us. It is difficult, nigh impossible, to find our new way in the midst of this racket. Eventually we remember silence. Only when we are still can we exchange the old for the new and discover a way to reemerge, letting in all sides of a quandary.

In silence I find the self who is my guide in the new world.

Birthdays

Less fuss made over my birthdays in my early life merits more fuss now, for I have outgrown the restraints of old family notions, and there is still plenty of time to celebrate this precious gift I have been given.

ISOBEL

Let us not number among the women who shy away from exposing their age. Let us instead boldly declare we are forty-five, fifty, fifty-five. Let us gather people together to celebrate these passing years, the arrival of our new challenges, the awareness of our wealth, the acknowledgment of our history.

Celebration is attention. It is important for each one of us to pay attention to this special day, the anniversary of the day on which we received life. We may feel childish for wanting a birthday party, but why not have one? It is not childish to turn to ourselves on our special day and heed exactly what we want and need. We are "coming to age" in each one of these years of our midlife. We are deep in transition and need to abide our instincts about the right form for our celebration.

I celebrate my birth each year in the way that is right for me.

Change

Every time I'm in for a major change, I think I'm dying.

ANONYMOUS

We say that cats have nine lives. Perhaps we do also. We are regularly dying from one change into the next one. Just as we think we have life mapped out for the long haul, we discover it is time to change again. Life's developmental stages are ever unfolding. When we were younger, we thought adulthood would level us out, offering a great plain on which to travel a flat straightaway. We did not realize just how much change an ongoing maturity demands.

Around our menopausal changes, many of us are drawn inward. We are sometimes dampened by depression. This may be the only way we can slow down enough to see the road signs that tell us more change is approaching.

Often the change we make in midlife is to afford more value to our inner life by altering our priorities and giving them more attention. Some of us start or return to therapy to receive guidance to look within. Some of us pursue a spiritual practice, spending more time listening to the wisdom within.

Change can feel more like birth than death, if I let it.

Poverty

I'm beginning to see that life after fifty or sixty is itself another country, as different as adolescence is from childhood, or the central years of life are from adolescence—and just as adventurous. At least it would be, if it weren't also a place of poverty for many, especially women over sixty-five, and of disregard for even more.

GLORIA STEINEM

Women as a group have traditionally been less economically independent than men. But we all deserve to be provided for and to understand how to manage our resources. Let us not let poverty steal from us what should be the adventurous journey into our older years. Let us begin providing for ourselves today, both through retirement savings and through educating ourselves about what we will need and how we will obtain it. And, when possible, let us help provide for other women.

Many of us have math anxiety. When it comes to looking at figures and trying to plan our financial future, we may cringe and give up easily, leaving it to our partner. Many women do not even know what they will receive in the event of the loss of their partner. Let us awaken ourselves and take notice in these matters. Even further, let us participate in providing what we need.

I pay attention now to providing for myself in the future.

Instinctual Nature

To adjoin the instinctual nature does not mean to come undone. . . . It means to establish territory, to find one's pack, to be in one's body with certainty and pride regardless of the body's gifts and limitations, to speak and act in one's behalf, to be aware, alert, to draw on the innate feminine powers of intuition and sensing, to come into one's cycles and protect them.

CLARISSA PINKOLA
ESTÉS, PH.D.

We fear our instinctual nature, associating it with the unrestrained animalistic expression we have been civilized out of. We fear that going to it will take us out of ourselves. But by Clarissa Pinkola Estés's description, it will take us into ourselves in the most profound way.

What does it mean "to come into one's cycles and protect them"? Surely menopause is one of our cycles. We protect it by refusing to deny it, by consciously coming to it. We look to the women among us who are Crones and recognize them as part of our pack. We establish the territory we need in order to undergo our changes—the inner space, the patience and respect we want to give our bodies.

Power rises within me when I adjoin my instinctual nature.

Loneliness

To me menopause is a lonely journey. I don't believe physicians know enough about how to alleviate the symptoms with an assurance of safety, and everyone goes through it differently anyway.

CAROL

Perhaps every experience in which one's body suddenly alters brings out loneliness, for even if we know others who are in the same condition, we feel alone in our bodies as we try to cope with what at first seems abnormal. We may be able to remember the loneliness that came with the arrival of our very first period. And haven't we felt lonely when we have faced illness or injury?

At least we are fortunate enough to be coming into menopause at a time when women are beginning to speak more openly about what they are encountering. It may help us feel less lonely to speak with others about our changes and about ways to cope with them. Sometimes our lonely feelings may be trying to tell us of our need to attend to a deeper part of ourselves that is being neglected. We may need to sit still with our loneliness until we discover those aspects that have long been kept in darkness but are now longing to emerge into the light.

Loneliness is a feeling passing through. I listen to its message.

Maturity

To mature is in part to realize that while complete intimacy and omniscience and power cannot be had, self-transcendence, growth, and closeness to others are nevertheless within one's reach.

SISSELA BOK

In youth we strive to stretch our limits. Sometimes this enlarges us; other times it merely frustrates us into learning lessons of humility and of our place in the world. We think: *This much power feels good, why not go for more?* When someone lets us close to them, we think our bond will not be complete until we know all of them. We are reluctant to leave some things alone, to simply be sated and believe that what we have is enough.

One of the pleasures of midlife is enjoying the rich texture that our relationships offer instead of wanting what they can't. Likewise with ourselves, when we concentrate on our growth, we derive great pleasure from seeing ourselves transcend old notions of who we thought we were allowed to be.

Today, I appreciate the ripening I enjoy from maturity.

Impostor

Another belief of mine: that everyone else my age is an adult, whereas I am in disguise.

MARGARET ATWOOD

A shocking number of us probably go around feeling as Margaret Atwood describes, as if we are in disguise. Perhaps we would do so less if we had welcoming rituals to carry us over into certain ages, if we did not live in a youth culture, and if we saw the expanding nature inherent in every age. Perhaps it is only natural that we are inclined to think we will be the exception and not age. Perhaps that is our way of holding to the innocent one in us, the one who only wants to catalog our experiences as they fit into an ideal picture.

Menopause is a leveler for our denial about aging. Perhaps we have had creaky joints for a year or more already, our hair has turned gray, and our skin has begun to seem as if it must belong to someone else, but we have not been paying attention. We have almost deliberately been looking the other way. Menopause offers us a distinct block of time in which to look more clearly at the place and time we have reached in life. Let us study ourselves in the mirror and join the pictures we have in our minds with these bodies before us now.

I don't wish to be an impostor. I grow into myself.

Solitude

After a few minutes of pleasant mental vacancy the creative thoughts begin to come. And these thoughts at first are found to be depressing, because the first thing they say is: What a senseless thing life is with nothing but talk, meals, reading, uninteresting work and listening to the radio. But that is . . . just where your imagination is leading you to see how life can be better.

BRENDA UELAND

If we never look at and admit our discontent, we are not motivated to redirect our energy to satisfy what is missing. And chances are, we cannot look at our discontent unless we are willing to spend some time alone.

For almost all of us it is frightening to enter our solitary times. It is as if we must step through a minefield before we can arrive at safe territory. No wonder then that we tend to keep busy and avoid making this journey for as long as possible. However, once we have walked through our fear and those first moments of depressing thoughts Brenda Ueland describes, we discover our creativity is alive and eager—to offer us ideas, to tell us what we need for the next stage of our fulfillment, and to give us our vitality.

Solitude can be frightening to reach, yet it provides all I need when I defy my fear to go there.

Cultural Differences

Studies show that Japanese women rarely experience hot flashes and other menopausal symptoms. Mayan women have virtually no menopausal complaints. Women in certain non-Western countries also manage to escape the degenerative diseases that plague American senior citizens: heart disease, cancer, and osteoporosis. How do they do it, and why can't we?

ELLEN BROWN AND LYNNE WALKER

In the United States, we tend to think we have it best when it comes to health care and medical advances. We do, in fact, have a high-caliber medical system and support much research. Yet this thinking can become solipsistic, keeping us from discovering other ways of being besides our own.

One of the great debates in our country is whether or not to take Estrogen Replacement Therapy. While this is an important debate, perhaps other factors also need more research. Perhaps other cultural influences, such as the common diet, exert profound effects upon the response of our bodies to menopause in the United States.

I open my mind to take a look at the way women experience menopause around the world.

Looking Forward

Paradoxical as it may seem, to believe in youth is to look backward; to look forward we must believe in age.

DOROTHY L. SAYERS

We must believe in age rather than in the false idea that we will be the exception who avoids it. We must also believe in the merits of age in order to be willing to look forward.

We all know the older woman who ceases growing into her life from middle age onward—the one who fails to let go of her children and wants to live through their lives, the one who madly seeks romance with younger men to prove to herself she is still attractive, the one who lives in nostalgia for her younger years, for the time when she felt she held more power. As this older woman ages, she grows more distant from herself, for her regret only grows as the inevitable arrives.

None of us need cling to youth. We each have an opportunity for a rich and rewarding aging. We only need to envision the life we want to grow into and begin to act to develop it.

I look forward eagerly to energize the age I am moving into.

Priestesses

The middle-aged, who have lived through their strongest emotions, but are yet in the time when memory is still half passionate and not merely contemplative, should surely be a sort of natural priesthood, whom life has disciplined and consecrated to be the refuge and rescue of early stumblers and victims of self-despair.

GEORGE ELIOT

Do we not have an obligation to serve as priestesses to the young? Is there any better way to receive awareness of our wisdom than by giving it away? There is not.

We have known the storm of emotions and have been brought close to our own shipwrecks. As we move through middle age we discover a new coolness in us, an ability to remain a bit detached as we watch ourselves be swayed by deep feelings. We notice our perspective is broader. This qualifies us to advise both ourselves and others more soundly, or as George Eliot suggests, "life has disciplined and consecrated [us] to be the refuge and rescue of early stumblers and victims of self-despair."

I offer to others that which I have gleaned through my earlier passages and seasoned with the exercise of time.

Finality

Never think you've seen
the last of anything.

EUDORA WELTY

Just as we assign finality to a relationship—"Ah, the family estate is settled. I'll be free of my greedy brother forever," or we leave a job that required working with someone who has been pushing our buttons—we discover the same situation repeating itself. We come to realize we are carrying a charged condition within us, and we merely find people or situations in the world to interact with it. Though we feel repelled by certain people, we are actually attracted to them, and if we don't pay attention this time round, they will simply pop up again to offer us another trial.

By midlife we learn to value making conscious closure with relationships that have ended, with other losses we have encountered, even with our own youth. Still, we understand that there is no black-and-white transition that separates us from our past and our youth. We carry all of this within us, even as we clear space for the future and place our energy where it will most benefit us today.

My urge toward finality is often an evasion of the forces that challenge me to further awaken to my life.

Consistency

She was the same through and through. You could go on cutting slice after slice and you knew you would never light upon a plum or a cherry or even a piece of peel.

KATHERINE MANSFIELD

Despite all the changes we manifest as we go through life, we discover certain characteristics that hold constant. Much of our nature came through at age two, and we are still that person. Looking through a photo album, we are struck by how clearly the essence of a person is seen from youth to old age.

By midlife, if we are still obsessed with the idea we want to be like someone else rather than who we are today, it is time to reckon with reality and look instead at why we are having difficulty accepting ourselves. It is important to tend to changing the behaviors we do not like in ourselves, but it is also important to learn to recognize our essence and sometimes leave ourselves alone.

I am the same through and through. I let this consistency characterize and stabilize me.

Envy

An envious heart makes
a treacherous ear.

ZORA NEALE
HURSTON

Envy is an emotion that darkens the heart and slips out in our shadow. We all feel it—for things that have passed us by but others have gotten. We often feel envy for lost things that will never be regained, most notably our youth. We project this with wistfulness upon the younger generation. Some of us envy our children the future still in front of them or even the very things we have made possible for them, such as a better education, foreign travel, or opportunities to express their artistic talents.

Often we are ashamed to admit envy, but envy admitted is less potent than envy denied. When we see and own our envy, we are able to contain it and sometimes even learn from it about just what we desire. When we disown it, our envy is likely to grow pushy and leak out, regardless of how tightly we think we are holding the lid down. It dampens our enthusiasm for the achievements of others and lessens our ability to partake of life.

I let my envy guide me to the places in my life where I need to make peace with myself.

Following Our Bodies

Beginning to follow my body rather than ordering it around after me was a major shift. But that wasn't all—the discovery that not everyone thought the same way about menstruation opened up my thinking. I began to realize that there was a wisdom inherent in the body itself and that my own culture didn't necessarily have a very wise or useful attitude to the processes of being female.

LARA OWEN

How many times have we tried to order our bodies around? Through menstruation and now through menopause we are given regular lessons in the falseness of this heavy-handed behavior. For certainly cramps never stopped because we commanded them to, and neither do our hot flashes. On the contrary, they show us just how distinctly autonomous our bodies can be.

When we stop resisting our bodies and begin listening to them, we discover their wisdom, most of which has been derided by contemporary Western culture. Some cultures have advocated respecting menstruation as a special time, even gathering women together for a time apart from other aspects of daily life. Some cultures advocate rest.

If we use our bodies as guides, they tell us at menopause: Go inward and be with the spirit of gestation.

I follow the voice that speaks wisely to me through my body.

Eternity

Eternity is not something that begins after you are dead. It is going on all the time. We are in it now.

CHARLOTTE PERKINS GILMAN

To think eternity begins at the moment of our death is to think that the world revolves around us. Rationally we know this cannot be true, and yet we begin as a baby whose original belief is that she is the center of the world. She is shocked in early life to discover this is not true. She spends most of her life letting go, bit by bit, of this innocent, all-embracing view.

As we mature, we no longer suffer over the reality that we are not the center of the universe. We can enjoy our humanity by taking a more humble view. We can more easily allow ourselves to make mistakes. We can let people come and go in our lives without trying to hold them captive. We do not always need to be striving for some superlative status, but we enjoy exactly where we find ourselves today in the realm of eternity.

My spirit belongs to eternity even while I am alive in this place and time in my body.

Mother's Daughter

The woman who bore me is no longer alive, but I seem to be her daughter in increasingly profound ways.

JONETTA B. COLE

We are deeply connected with our mothers, even when we consciously try to reject them and make much of not being like them. In midlife we often notice ourselves repeating their sayings. We see them when we look in the mirror. We hear them in our thoughts about aging.

Some of our mothers were withholding, neglectful, or otherwise downright negative toward us as an expression of their own unfulfilled desires. We who are their daughters may hold a resentment against them, which spoils any pleasure in our resemblances. Often at the time of their death or thereafter, realizing that their limitations were acquired from the treatment of an earlier generation, we are able to experience forgiveness. Then our fonder memories come through, and we are able to take strength from the steely parts of our mothers and go forward from them.

Today, as her daughter, I proudly carry the legacy of my mother.

Minority Power

Every effort for progress, for enlightenment, for science, for religious, political, and economic liberty, emanates from the minority, and not from the mass.

EMMA GOLDMAN

We who are openly concerned about aging and the way it is affected by ageism are a minority. But let us not be discouraged by that. For as Emma Goldman points out, minorities are always the instigators of progress.

Many of us have already partici-pated in movements that have seen great changes in our life-times—the civil rights movement, the women's movement, the peace movement, the struggle for gay and lesbian rights. Our wheels are oiled. We need only direct our attention and give our energy to those who have already begun to address ageism, such as the Gray Panthers, and bring this conscious-ness into our daily lives.

We start within ourselves by rejecting the dominant view—the attitude that devalues us for aging and ignores us just when we are becoming richly valuable in our wisdom. We hold steadfast to our wisdom and insist on making room for its due.

I make great strides for myself and all others by joining the minority who insist upon the changes that will cradle my existence.

Sexuality

> You know the mind *is* an astonishing, long-living, erotic thing.
>
> **GRACE PALEY**

The mind lives as long as we do and is our most vital sexual organ, always playing a major role during sexual arousal, provoking excitement in others and within ourselves. Our mind cannot escape the influence of our society's notions about aging, including the idea that our sexuality keeps drying up with each year "over the hill."

Indeed, as we grow older most of us do encounter some changes in our sexuality. We may feel less driven by its urges. We may encounter physical changes that lead us to give more time and attention to foreplay. We may require lubricants to relieve vaginal dryness. But none of these needs will turn us away from our sexuality unless we let the negative voices in our mind overwhelm our feelings of desire.

Let us keep our minds open to desire, which never shrivels up or is out of commission. Our sexuality is something that we carry with us right up to our death. Let us keep its expression alive in whatever manner we find enlivening.

Today, I enjoy the presence of my sexuality.

Faith

Who has seen the wind?
Neither you nor I:
But when the trees bow
down their heads,
The wind is passing by.

CHRISTINA ROSSETTI

Faith is nothing more than holding fast to a belief system when we can only see oblique evidence that would verify and validate it. Many of us, without even being aware of it, cling fiercely to a faith in negative beliefs, such as the notion that we are unlovable or that others want to hurt us. Why not turn our focus to having faith in a more positive view, one that inspirits us and lets us know hope?

At midlife, it is wise to ask ourselves what we have put our faith in. Do we believe that a higher order of guidance exists that is greater than our own will? Do we conduct ourselves as if we believe it? Are we aware that this belief is a choice, as is believing that things happen randomly? We are free to make new choices at any time on our journey.

My faith often carries me when the road gets rough.

Creativity

Creativity is like a great
receptive womb.

LYNN V. ANDREWS

There is an expanse of creativity in each of us. Most of us have discovered some of its outlines by midlife—that it lies in wait for us to quiet down enough to feel its pulse; that rather than being stuck in the black and white of things, it holds the potential to arrive at the fresh option, the enlightened or transforming option; that it always desires expression and will turn to longing unless we attend to and nurture it.

Menopause is a time to reflect upon our receptivity. If we have put forth a great tide of extroverted energy until now, we may be only vaguely familiar with the quieter, more receptive aspect of ourselves. We may feel frightened to drop away what feels like a safer exterior to even see what lies within. But let us rest assured that our creativity waits as long as is needed and will meet us when we are ready to greet it and draw it from its womb.

*I touch the creativity held womblike inside of me and
see that it is ever present, awaiting my attention.*

Self-realization

The dream is real, my friends. The failure to realize it is the only unreality.

TONI CADE BAMBARA

Everything we want to do or be starts with a dream, a vision. Sometimes this dream seems a very far distance from reality, yet without it how would we have known to begin walking in a certain direction?

When we put our dreams off as unreal or meaningless, they come back again and again to try and prompt us. Eventually they may dry up from lack of attention. But as soon as we give them a nod of recognition, they once again provide a landscape on which we can cast our imagination.

Midlife gives us a chance to reassess what is real to us. What are we honoring? What have we realized in ourselves and what visions have we ignored because they seemed too remote to us? Midlife tells us to look again and let our dreams happen.

I look back and notice how many of my dreams have become real with time.

Timing

You can't push a wave onto the shore any faster than the ocean brings it in.

SUSAN STRASBERG

Life's forces have their own deep rhythms. We are only privy to hints about how much of the timing we can control. This is one of the ways we grow wiser with middle age. We learn to let go faster when we find we are pushing a wave and getting no results for our efforts. We learn to shift our focus if we are exerting ourselves uselessly.

Still, we often resist. We get caught up thinking we will fail if we don't keep pushing harder or longer. We try to build our muscles when the answer lies elsewhere—perhaps in our spiritual development. We become frustrated because there can be little peace within us if we are driving against the flow of life's forces. What a relief when at last we decide to let go and give ourselves over to the flow and timing of greater forces.

The time frame of my will often drives me relentlessly.
I surrender it and trust that all I need will come
to me in its right time.

Convergence

Each life converges to
some centre
Expressed or still.

EMILY DICKINSON

Convergence is a useful way to think of the midlife years. In youth we have the impulse to open our arms wide and travel down many roads, both literally and figuratively. We cannot discover our center without exploration, for there is much we discover within only by finding a representative for it in the outer world. For instance, we might discover our affinity for psychology when we take our first psychology course; we might find out we love painting by being drawn to other painters.

By midlife we may feel lost if we have not also begun to converge toward our center. We may feel plagued with longing or the sensation that life is passing us by. It is a good time to seek out whatever help we need to bring us toward our center.

However, it is not as if our alarm clock has gone off, and we must stop one section of our life and begin another. We continue to converge toward our center until the moment of our death. We also continue to explore, and this, too, brings us closer.

Today, I delight in the ways I am converging toward my center.

Aging

Younger people can't tell us that we aren't old; we know better. Is my body the shapely one I see in this photograph of a young woman sitting on the edge of a swimming pool forty years ago? Far from it. What's more, I don't know when the process of irrefutable aging began; I didn't notice until it was too late. The screws of old age turn so slyly that it takes you by surprise.

MARY MEIGS

Often we still have the picture of the young woman of forty years ago or of twenty years ago in our mind's eye. Then at certain points, menopause being perhaps the most notable one, we make a leap forward. After that leap, when younger people try to tell us that we aren't aging, we cease to be charmed by this. It becomes a denial of our reality. While we don't exactly relish aging, we do want to be who we are.

Perhaps some of our surprise at aging and the way it sneaks up on us is related to the gradually developing visceral awareness of our mortality. This puts a new perspective on the meanings of our lives. We are probably less important in the grand scheme of things than we once thought we were. We are probably more important, too.

Surprise at my age tells me to slow down and appreciate myself.

Destruction

Those who cannot live
fully often become
destroyers of life.

ANAÏS NIN

We have all seen parents and grandparents who could not give to their children or grandchildren what they were not able to have themselves, who never ceased competing with the very ones they wanted to love. Perhaps they wanted an education, but there was no opportunity for them to go to school; they had to work to support a family instead. When it came time for them to encourage their children, they were filled with ambivalence and often sabotaged the efforts of their children, even though they meant to support them.

As we move into midlife, let us examine the places where our lives have not become full. Let us know that now is not too late to change things; rather now is the ideal time. We can still go to school. We can still become an artist. We can still have the relationship we yearn for. Let us turn to face whatever holds us apart from achieving our desires and cease being destroyers.

*I fill out the empty spaces in my life that otherwise
lead me to be destructive.*

Love

There is always something left to love. If you ain't learned that, you ain't learned nothing.

LORRAINE HANSBERRY

Those of us who are single in midlife may grow discouraged about love. Perhaps we have lost a long-term love. Perhaps we have gone through a painful separation, which has left us feeling betrayed in our loving: We gave our all, we truly loved this person, and yet, ultimately, we were deeply injured. Why would we want to love again?

Part of our midlife maturation is to come to terms with the notion that though love sometimes hurts it is still worthwhile. In fact, more than merely worthwhile, it is a vital part of spiritual sustenance.

We need not have a lover to love. There is always someone to love, first and foremost ourselves. Let us think of ourselves as a channel for the flow of love, both its receiver and its giver. As we release our love freely, we also regain confidence in letting others love us.

I learn today that there is plenty to love, and I am alive as love's conduit.

Independence

You come into the world alone and you go out of the world alone yet it seems to me you are more alone while living than even going and coming.

EMILY CARR

Why squander our time worrying about whether we will be alone in our older years when we can appreciate our independence regardless of our circumstances? For true independence is our ability to enter our own lives fully.

We are meant to be interdependent with others, learning from them, giving of ourselves to them, listening and sharing with them, but at our core we still remain independent beings. As women we are often reluctant to accept this. We may feel as if our existence is reflected primarily in who we are to others. We have been taught to think this. Yet we are only ourselves. Let us not be reluctant to be independent.

Independence does not cut me off from others;
it gives me a firm ground from which
to reach them.

Lostness

When we are lost in empty lives, it's hard to hear the instinctual voice . . . that tells us almost in a whisper the great secret—that the trials of our most disorienting experiences are slowly working on us to transform our consciousness. It's as if we were caught in a vestibule between an old way of being and a new.

JANE R. PRÉTAT

As we grow older we may develop an expectation that we will no longer have peaks and valleys in our psychic landscape, that we will have a smooth, gradual uphill journey with self-knowledge being revealed to us regularly along the way, as if life were a time-release capsule. We may be in for disappointment or surprise when life doesn't meet our expectations.

In fact the more common way we move through a transition is first to arrive at a place in which we feel lost. Some old ways are no longer working for us; we shed them but have nothing to take their place. We may regress to childish behavior. We may grow depressed and have trouble simply getting out of bed. We may feel as if we are wandering aimlessly in a forest, or as if we have been cast adrift on a raft with no ability to steer. Our greatest challenge in the midst of these feelings is to hear our instinctual voice with its message of transformation. We are on our way to being born anew.

I listen in lostness and learn to trust my instinctual voice.

Realization

The inner experience consolidates, and instead of being a kind of emotional spiritual experience, it becomes a realization in the most literal sense of the word. We use the word "realization" rather too lightly; but if we "realize" something in its basic meaning, it becomes a real thing forever.

MARIE-LOUISE VON FRANZ

How often do we trust that changes we have made will stick? Many of us have a basic fear that realizations come and go, and when we come to a new insight, we grasp it for the moment but do not have much faith that it will consolidate within us.

Menopause is a good time for us to reverse this belief in the fickleness of our growth, for menopause is a time of consolidating our wisdom. Our blood hereafter will be held within us, as will a new integration of what we have learned of life so far. We have much more to learn, but we can take pleasure in knowing that what has already been "realized" by us is now our foundation. We stand upon it without floundering. We let it be a source of confidence in ourselves.

I believe in the reality of those things I have realized.

Bliss

The bliss that comes from ignorance should seldom be encouraged for it is like to do one out of a more satisfying bliss.

RUTH STOUT

Aren't we often seeking bliss avidly enough that we are willing to accept the version that comes with ignorance? Each time we reach a plateau of some comfort we wish to remain there as long as possible. Denial helps us ignore our yet untended business. Why not just stay there forever?

Because we do not know what we are missing. Also, if we try to maintain an equilibrium based on ignorance, we are likely to hurt others around us.

The more satisfying bliss beyond the bliss of our ignorance holds the power to unify us and put us into harmony with the universe. No one is doing us a favor if they help us to stay in a state below this. We deserve the very best, including a taste of true bliss.

I give up false attachments to a bliss based in ignorance and let myself move on to the real thing.

Ripening

I've never heard anything about how a woman feels who is going to have a child, or about how a pear tree feels bearing its fruit. I would like to read these things many years from now, when I am barren and no longer trembling like this.

MERIDEL LESUEUR

We must describe our moments of ripening and how they mark our lives for all to see and know. They come not only with childbearing but at every stage of life in different forms. For instance, at menopause many of us feel as if we are in a cocoon of gestation, ripening for the years ahead—for receiving the wisdom of our older self and for expressing whatever is yet unlived in us.

How do we feel as we ripen? We gather up force and abundance as one gathers up the harvest. We feel growth occurring inside of us, as perhaps we once felt the formation of a child growing in us. We feel the timing of nature, learning to put aside our own urges to hurry things and wait for a moment of delivery. We feel anticipation of splendor. And finally, we feel the satisfaction of birth, in this case our renewal.

I chart the feelings of ripening as they occur within me.

Fulfillment

Breath is life, and the intermingling of breaths is the purpose of good living. This is in essence the great principle on which all productive living must rest, for relationships among all the beings of the universe must be fulfilled; in this way each individual life may also be fulfilled.

PAULA GUNN ALLEN

If we do not feel fulfilled, let us look to our relationships with other beings, both to human beings and to plants and animals. For we are all interdependent. Are we breathing freely and letting ourselves resonate with the way our breath intermingles with that of others? Or have we contracted our breath, pulling ourselves back from life to try to protect against the injuries that sometimes come with our interactions.

Let us become full participants. Rather than entering the arena of life fully armed with demands and expectations, let us think of intermingling. Let us thank a tree for its existence. Let us touch a friend with the care we feel in our heart for them. Let us receive the love of our pets when they come to rub against us.

My day is filled with interaction, if I recognize my interdependence with all the other beings around me.

Making Use

I looked at the quilt on the car seat next to me, thinking how women have always saved and pieced together the castoffs, pioneer women having to use and reuse every scrap of cloth, so that a woman might cut up a feedsack and make trousers of it; then, when they were worn out, a dress for the baby; then rags and headscarves; until finally the remaining pieces she would stitch into the pattern of a quilt.

SANDY BOUCHER

We come from a long tradition of women who know how to make use, over time, of a thing like a piece of cloth, which comes to its final resting place in a quilt, giving joy to whoever looks at it.

We can do the same with our lives as they change over time. When our physical vigor wanes a bit, we can recut the cloth and make ourselves a new garment, perhaps by learning to do the same things in a manner that conserves our energy, perhaps by resting from physical exertion but tuning up our energy in other realms, such as the spiritual or the intellectual. We can take the same cloth, which is our essence, and use it in a new way.

I make use of my energy today in a way that fits me well.

Belly Fat

I never had a belly before. Now I've grown one. It's kind of cute. It's big enough to rest on my thighs when I lean forward. It's smooth and soft. It's my midlife pregnancy. I wonder what surprises it is going to deliver me.

JULIE

Our bodies do tend to gain weight around the middle at midlife. According to many sources, weightier women tend to have an easier time of menopause with fewer hot flashes. Fat cells produce some estrogen. Thin women tend to have greater problems with osteoporosis.

We must make our own choices regarding weight gain and whether we want to fight against it or allow it. If we do have a newly grown or expanded belly, we might look at it with the attitude Julie takes. What surprises does it hold for us? Can we center on it as a storehouse for our gestating Crone, the wisdom integrating within us? Can we cease pining for our younger body and love the one we have as it changes?

Today, I give my body, with all its parts, a loving embrace.

Composting the Past

She seems to have had the ability to stand firmly on the rock of her past while living completely and un-regretfully in the present.

MADELEINE L'ENGLE

To make good use of the past is no less an exhilarating accomplishment than to make good compost. In the spring we dig the dark loam that forms from remnants left behind, unconsumed, mixed together with decaying leaves and twigs. We offer this fertilizer to our garden, turning it in with the soil. By this time of the year a wealth of vegetables and flowers assures us of the abundant giving of the cycle.

The parts of our past that are no longer useful to us must be set aside and left behind. They become waste, and yet they need not be wasted, for they go into the sum of our experience. They become part of the good soil that helps us grow today. It is only when we fail to let them go and try to preserve them that the inevitable decay spoils our new efforts, making us feel that we are hopelessly destined to repeat the same patterns.

With the past as my soil, I am free to encounter the present.

Spirituality

The liberating encounter with God/ess is always an encounter with our authentic selves resurrected from underneath the alienated self. It is not experienced against, but in and through relationships, healing our broken relations with our bodies, with other people, with nature.

ROSEMARY RUETHER

While we once might have elevated the spiritual to a lofty height, detached from our bodies and from our relationships with others, by midlife we know enough to recognize the presence of our spirit in mundane and everyday life.

We are always seeking to meet up more fully with our authentic selves. We do this through healing our old wounds, which are often uncovered by our current relationships. In the midst of healing these wounds, we have a hard time believing that we are engaged in a spiritual process. Yet over and over we discover that we are. We are related to all human beings and to all of nature, and we discover ourselves through the manifestation of our conduct with all beings.

I see how my spirit underlies all growth in my life.

Depression

Depression is not an easy companion on your journey, but let her go with us for a while. In her bundle, she carries the anger you have carefully frozen with frigid blasts of fear and kept nourished with your pain. Dare to accept her bundle, to accept your own wholeness. Dare to forgive what hurt you and stop reliving the pain. Dare to thaw your rage.

GRANDMOTHER GROWTH (SUSUN S. WEED)

Many of us encounter bouts of depression at different junctures in our lives. Recent studies show that the incidence of depression is greater in women whose menopause has been induced, and that in women who achieve menopause naturally, it is probably no greater than the normal incidence of depression in women.

In feeling our way through depression, let us locate our anger and see if it is strangulating us. Let us feel the fear that keeps us from dealing with it. Often we are keeping a lid on a powder keg, and perhaps the depression wants to tell us: "Get to the bottom of this, for your vitality is being stolen by your anger." We all have wounds. Until we allow ourselves to feel our indignation, they will not be able to heal. Let us find the support we need to do the work, so that we can release our vitality into every part of our being.

I walk with my depression today to where it wants to lead me.

Flexibility

> Misfortune had made Lily supple instead of hardening her, and a pliable substance is less easy to break than a stiff one.
>
> **EDITH WHARTON**

We think of rigidity as something that comes with age. We speak of others or of ourselves as becoming set in our ways, of having developed lifelong habits, such as what we eat, how we sleep, and how we feel about things. Though our bodies do, in fact, lose some of the suppleness of youth, we shouldn't make the mistake of imagining that all aspects of us are losing suppleness.

If we do think this way, we may fail to see the parts of us that are becoming more pliable. A vital feature of wisdom is a slackening rigidity. While we felt assured of what we knew in youth, we now find ourselves more open to not knowing. While we once thought a major blow would throw us completely off balance, we now know our balance comes from some place deeper within. We are now much more like the weeping willow. When the wind blows we bend, and when it stops we straighten again without pause.

I appreciate the flexibility I have gained with age and experience.

Stories

The universe is made of stories, not of atoms.

MURIEL RUKEYSER

We are wise to listen to the stories that make up the universe and our own lives as well. In our mothers' generation, at least in white America, too much of the story of menopause was made up by doctors. Women were silenced about their actual experiences; they spoke in whispers when they spoke at all. Rarely was pen put to paper to record what it was like for them.

It is difficult to know the present when the past has been obscured, made invisible or distorted. Our work now is to share our stories with one another and to write them down. We can also look far back to matriarchal times to find the stories that reveal the power and wisdom of the Crone. These, too, are ours and make up our world like atoms, if we are aware of them. We need their strength as we make our place as women elders in a world that affords little visibility or respect to elders.

Today, I am free to speak and write the story of my menopause, filling in the gaps in the story of the universe.

Acceptance of Talents

*I've accepted my reality.
I was meant to sound
the way I do.*

KATHLEEN BATTLE

A certain amount of self-esteem is required to accept the talents we have been given and to develop the ability to express them. When we are lacking this self-esteem, we think too little of our talents and abilities. Even when we accomplish something outstanding, we minimize it as soon as it is done, thinking if *we* could do it, then anyone could, even though rationally we know this is not true.

By midlife we are more likely to have an honest and accurate picture of ourselves and our talents. If we have not come to accept them, this becomes one of our priorities. For when we deny our skills and special abilities and the pleasure and satisfaction they offer to others, we come up empty when we should be full. We deny ourselves our connection to the sources of our gifts, and we act as if we are barren when we are actually fecund.

Just as I would not want other women to deny their talents, I accept mine and appreciate my ability to express them.

Meeting the World

It is possible to practice meeting the world, rather than regarding it as an object of knowledge, to leave behind the desire to appropriate experience, and begin to think in terms of relation.

CAROLYN FORCHÉ

When we think in terms of relation, it helps us to remain humble. We see ourselves as precious and unique individuals, but we also see that we exist in the context of a greater design. We let ourselves be in the moment of our experience without comparing it to other times, people, or places. We don't say to ourselves, "The past was better than this," "This person is not good enough for me," "This person is above me," or "It would be better if I were in some other place."

To enter into relation is to court intimacy, and with that comes the attendant possibility of being wounded. We cannot relate without becoming vulnerable to how something may affect us. We might be hurt by any person we choose to relate to. We might be touched by them as well and moved along on our journey. When we enter into relation, we open to the unknown.

I meet the world rather than trying to make it mine.

Experiencing Aging

What was she going to experience? Nothing much more than, simply, she grew old: that successor and repetition of the act of growing up. It happens to everyone, of course ... *Ah me, time flies!* ... *Before you know it, life has gone past* ... *Ripeness is all.*

DORIS LESSING

Aging is perhaps the most insidious of all processes. It happens before our eyes but so subtly that often it seems to have happened without our awareness. It is important to awaken to it as much as we possibly can, for we do not like being suddenly jolted by the notion that our life has gone past without our noticing it.

What do we experience as we go through midlife? Growing up further—our growth as enlargement, like an iris that continues to divide and foster new shoots.

We no longer serve the purposes of our younger lives, whether that meant raising our children or discovering what values were important to us and where we could connect and express ourselves in the world. We grow into contentment with ourselves as adults, letting life become more precious as it passes.

My life continues to expand as I grow older.

Resources

[In times of crisis] if we are lucky, we are able to call every resource, every forgotten image that can leap to our quickening, every memory that can make us know our power. And this luck is more than it seems to be: it depends on the long preparation of the self to be used.

MURIEL RUKEYSER

The older we become, the greater the supply of resources we have within, available to be called upon in our moments of need. Often we only recognize this preparedness during or after a crisis.

Sometimes we fear we are weakening and becoming less resourceful with age. Our bones are thinning. So is our memory. How will we possibly respond in a solid way when next we are presented with a major problem?

When the problem does come, we are given an opportunity to appreciate the wealth of our past. We remember how we have faced other crises. A clear vision of our purpose gives us a strong posture and emboldens us. Even our vulnerability lends us strength, since we know we aren't faking anything.

I appreciate how my years offer me a preparedness that is there when I call upon it.

Growth

The truth is that, like every other part of nature, human beings have an internal imperative to grow.

GLORIA STEINEM

By midsummer in certain climates we are presented with high growth. Many of us are awed to discover cucumbers, zucchini, and green beans growing on green plants we not long ago planted as seeds. All around us we see the mandate of nature is *growth*.

Our midlife is no less a period for growth than any other life season. Is it a time for pulling inward to manifest our changes? Yes, but that inward movement is like the seed gestating before its upward growth.

In our aging we are ever growing, not shrinking or disappearing. With awareness we can revel in the growth that comes with each new day and appreciate the harvest of seeds planted in earlier years.

Today, I gladly accept nature's mandate to grow.

Doubt

Faith and doubt both are needed—not as antagonists, but working side by side—to take us around the unknown curve.

LILLIAN SMITH

Faith carries us across the rough passages. Doubt keeps us awake and aware. Without doubt we are lulled into a sleepy state in which we take things for granted.

For instance, in midlife doubts may arise about whether we are fulfilling our purpose or about our ambition to achieve a certain position or level of accomplishment in life. Did we set our goals beyond our reach? Do we now have to scale back and settle for less or persevere in our quest? Our doubts help us reassess, considering our limits and examining our motives. Balanced by faith in our process, we find ourselves more comfortable living with the ambivalent feelings our doubts may arouse. Our goals are not necessarily scaled back but appear more attainable when we cease to demand their fulfillment.

Today, I appreciate balanced doses of faith and doubt.

Choice

I used to think to grow up I had to be content with sacrificing certain things to have others. Now I see it's more a matter of choice. When I choose what matters to me, the rest falls away.

MARY

When we find ourselves overly busy and cranky and we stop to examine what is wrong, we usually discover we are caught up in a cycle of responding to other people's needs or to our own unconscious impulses. Perhaps we have forgotten that at every moment we have the opportunity to make choices, to appraise our lives coolly and say: Yes, this will satisfy my needs; no, that will not.

Making choices gives us our power—not the kind of power that oppresses someone else but the power that comes from within. Sometimes we feel deeply pulled in opposite directions. For instance, perhaps we are attracted to someone who repeatedly withdraws from us. Does this mean this person doesn't want to start a relationship? Or is this how this person reacts in a situation that requires intimacy? We can make the choice to go toward or away from this person at each opportunity. Sometimes we have to persevere and stay close to this person long enough to understand our attraction before we can choose to move away. So long as we are choosing, we will not become a victim.

I sacrifice nothing today, but I do make choices.

Earth

> I get energy from the earth itself, and I get optimism from the earth itself. I feel that as long as the earth can make a spring every year, I can. As long as the earth can flower and produce nurturing fruit, I can, because I'm the earth. I won't give up until the earth gives up.
>
> **ALICE WALKER**

The earth withstands many blows, some wreaked by nature, like floods and earthquakes, some wreaked by humankind's careless use of her resources. And yet she comes back with another spring. In fact a deeper frost sometimes impels her to offer a more glorious spring than ever before.

We, too, withstand our blows. We lose our parents and other loved ones. We encounter illnesses that limit us and call forth our deepest resources. We face disillusionment and disappointments about people and things that are out of our control; we cannot escape the despair that comes with this. During our darkest hours, we do not feel as if we will ever blossom again. But of course we do. We make a return, just as we see the earth do. And after each descent, we come back a little fuller.

I take inspiration from the earth and her continuing demonstrations of renewal.

Limits

It is the denial of death that is partially responsible for people living empty, purposeless lives; for when you live as if you'll live forever, it becomes easy to postpone the things you know that you must do.

ELISABETH KÜBLER-ROSS

Death provides a boundary to life, and boundaries help us fulfill our purpose. In youth we tend to deny death. Perhaps from time to time we are confronted with the death of someone we know and then we are forced to recognize it, but still we may think of that occurrence as an exception, an anomaly. We have an ambivalent relationship with limits in general. We need help with discipline and at the same time resent any authority who sets limits for us.

By midlife, we usually look at limits quite differently. We appreciate the value of the containment of limits. We realize we choose many of the boundaries we function within, and they help us to move toward our goals without procrastination. Other boundaries, such as death, are beyond our control, but these, too, help to contain and motivate us, as long as we accept them.

My awareness and acceptance of death helps me to keep the important elements of my life in the foreground and not get lost in the details.

Hot Flashes

My fifties have been dominated by menopause, and I think there really isn't any way for women to prepare for it. Hot flashes are very real! . . . I've had them for five years now, just about every forty minutes. I found that there is a connection between a brief feeling of despair, like what I went through when I was depressed in my twenties.

ALLIE LIGHT

Allie Light experienced each hot flash preceded by a fifteen- to twenty-second period of depression, leading her to believe the depression of her youth was chemically based. It is of great value to us all to have her experience recorded. The more we are able to read of the experiences of individual women, the less daunting menopause becomes. Finding our own experience recorded, we cease to feel so alone with it, and this, in itself, lightens our burden.

Women have a wide variety of experiences with hot flashes. Some women seem to have night sweats exclusively, others have a few hot flashes a month, and others have one every twenty minutes. Most of us have had some episode before we reach menopausal age that resembles a hot flash—a time when our thermostat dysfunctioned, during or preceding a period or during some other illness.

I am grateful to those who speak and write about their hot flashes.

Deeds

Our deeds still travel
with us from afar,
And what we have been
makes us what we are.

GEORGE ELIOT

Our deeds add up to make us who we are today. All of us have our misdeeds, too. Perhaps we treated others badly, taking out our anger on them. Perhaps we neglected someone we meant to love. We are only human, and it is in our nature to sometimes err and commit misdeeds. But once we forgive ourselves for them, though they remain a part of our past, they no longer hold the power to haunt us.

Now, in midlife, we are more conscious of how our deeds are chosen daily. Our actions are not arbitrary or capricious or taken because of the influence of someone else. We are at the helm, making the choices.

We need only consider the day ahead of us and determine what deeds we shall choose. Perhaps we will make a greater effort to be appreciative of our closest friends and family, as a gesture of our love and respect for those who support us daily. Perhaps we will begin to fulfill some desire we have been putting aside and ignoring. Let us note at the end of the day the good feeling that derives from carrying out our chosen deeds.

My deeds are simple beads that, together, form a fine necklace.

Maturity

Youth is the time when one's whole life is entangled in a web of identity. . . . Not until life has passed through that retarded channel out upon the wide open sea of impersonality, can one really begin to live, not simply with the intenser part of oneself, but with one's entire being.

ELLEN GLASGOW

In youth we believe if only we had a stronger sense of our identity, we could live with our entire being. We seek it through association with our peers, through rebellion from our families, and through discovering our own interests and affinities.

Later we discover that a full life is more than a strong identity. We discover we have spent a lot of self-focused time trying to be less self-focused, until finally we adopt the view that we are not so important after all. At the same time we know we are extremely important. We come to this naturally with age. As we reconcile ourselves with our mortality, our unique personal identity fades, and we become more entirely alive without the need to be the center of the universe.

I function from a broader place than my identity.

Passing

All right for Chrissie to claim old age. But Margaret knew that she, herself, looked sixty, maybe fifty-five. Dr. Branson had said that, completely unsolicited, at her last check-up. So she got away with it. Got away with putting ten years less on her forms. Got away with indigo hair at age seventy.

VALERIE MINER

We ask ourselves why shouldn't we pass for younger if we are able to? What do we have to lose? Passing always exacts a price. It leaves us standing on a shaky foundation. It leaves us unable to organize and stand up for ourselves because our energy is diverted into pretending we are not who we are. Furthermore, it can even keep us from recognizing ourselves.

Imagine how shocking the prevalence of breast cancer would be if every woman who had had a mastectomy stopped wearing her prosthesis for a week. While we must each make our own choices regarding our appearance, let us always be mindful that we are trading one sort of power (the power of showing fully who we are) for another (the power we gain by appearing more acceptable to our society).

Rather than gloating at my abilities to pass, I consider the costs of passing, too.

Accepting Transition

I was in the mirror looking for the gray hairs, looking for the wrinkles, looking at my body. I guess I expected this deterioration to be instantaneous. It was vanity, because really I wasn't worried about anything else because the rest of my life is exciting. I don't feel the constraints. . . . I'm not worried about what this one says, or that one; it's breaking me out of my shell.

LEOTA LONE DOG

Don't we all do this as we reach midlife? Start searching and cataloging changes? Worry that there's going to be a sudden transition, and we're not ready for it? One month we do not have a period, and we think, "Now it is going to be all over quickly," but still the transition delivers itself slowly. Chances are our periods return for another showing. Our skin dries up, appears more opaque, then another day it again looks like younger skin. It takes a while for us to observe and accept this journey.

Meanwhile we are just fine, appreciating like Leota Lone Dog the ways in which our lives are expanding, enjoying the greater ease of living that comes with being more confident about caring for ourselves and what we think and worrying less about others.

My midlife transition offers peaks and valleys. I learn to be less extreme in my reactions to them.

Pessimism

Dwelling on the negative simply contributes to its power.

SHIRLEY MACLAINE

When obstacles present themselves, we must respond to them. It does not do to simply avert our eyes and ignore them. Nor does it do to get caught up in dwelling on negative possibilities. Sometimes we think that if we worry a problem enough, continually putting ourselves through the worst possible scenario, then we will be unscathed if that scenario comes to pass. But this worrying is no real preparation. It only wears us down.

In preparing for or encountering menopause, we are challenged to concentrate on the positive, especially since the history of recent generations has dwelled on the negative. We must take in the imaginative power of the Crone rather than the aging woman over the hill—"the old bag." Let us give our power to the positive possibilities that are imminent in our future—the fruits of our ripening, the flow of our creative juices, the integration of our wisdom.

I recognize problems and obstacles but focus on the positive solutions.

Fair Measure

Someone, I tell you,
will remember us.

We are oppressed by
fear of oblivion

SAPPHO

Some of us have difficulty believing that what we have done adds up to a life that matters. We fear if we disappear tomorrow we will be forgotten. Our marks will be quickly erased. Our achievements will not have lasting value.

Looking at our contributions through a positive lens, we see they are substantial. Developing ourselves, working to benefit ourselves and others, bringing our children into the world and showing up for them over many years to the best of our abilities—these are meritorious acts for which we can love and laud ourselves.

We need not fear oblivion. We need only count ourselves in fair measure for our worth.

Reflecting back over my achievements today, I notice how generously they add up.

Wonder

The more I wonder . . .
the more I love.

ALICE WALKER

In children, we can see the wondrous beings that we all are. If we can't remember this aspect of ourselves from our childhoods, we can look to the children in our lives now. We can watch them discover and examine new things. We can see their delight in magic when a rabbit miraculously appears from nowhere.

What happens as we grow older to dampen our sense of wonder? We begin to believe that to be in charge we must be able to control things. The unknown becomes more annoying than fascinating. We tend to block out the mysteries that come with uncertainty. Ultimately we discover that this makes us feel lifeless.

We can regain our sense of wonder whenever we want to. As soon as we are receptive, Nature—whether through plants, animals, or fellow human beings—will awe and embrace us and lead us to know love.

I reclaim wonder and give myself the gift of its vision.

Purpose

I begin to have an idea of my life, not as the slow shaping of achievement to fit my preconceived purposes, but as the gradual discovery and growth of a purpose which I didn't know.

JOANNA FIELD

With the arrogance of youth, we are often sure that we know what is right for us. If only this impediment or that one would get out of our way, we complain. If only we could reach our goal faster. Many times when our will is strongly driving us to chase these things, we confuse our efforts with the notion that we are fulfilling our purpose.

By midlife we have achieved some of our more superficial or material goals. Yet we desire *more*—not more of the same but a reaching further. Perhaps now we are ready to be quiet enough to listen to the guidance leading us to our deeper purposes. Perhaps we can accept the slow unfolding that comes mysteriously as we go beyond our will and seek the will of a greater force in the universe.

I open myself to a fuller discovery of my purposes on this planet.

Self-care

All my life I took care of others and did it well. You would think that would qualify me for taking care of myself, but it doesn't. When it comes to me, I am often a lost cause.

GINNY

Learning to take good care of oneself is a life-long, ever-expanding journey that branches into many realms. Perhaps we've lavished nourishment on our children but have rarely turned the same energy on ourselves. Perhaps we've taken good care of ourselves economically, but when it came to making time for our spirits, we've been neglectful, afraid to be alone and quiet enough to listen.

It is time to turn our attention to those neglected areas. Rather than saying, "That's just not my thing," or "I'll leave that to others who know how to do it," we can begin a fledgling exploration and experimentation. Despite being middle-aged, we must be willing to be young and untried in some areas. By humbling ourselves to the truth of what we don't know, we become eminently teachable and receive the joy of learning.

I open to new ways of learning to care for myself.

Spirituality

I found God in myself
and I loved her fiercely.

NTOZAKE SHANGE

Many of us grew up within an organized religion but developed little sense
of God within us. Often we became
alienated and moved away from this foundation, paying little
or no attention to our spiritual needs. We lived in the secular
world, seeking our satisfaction in the personal and perhaps
the political realms.

Eventually we may have begun longing for the spiritual
dimension and sought an image of God and/or Goddess that
would be right for us—a God of our understanding. We have
discovered we do not need to look far; we can look within.
Whether we define God as love, or soul, or our connecting
spirit—as the part of us connected to higher wisdom—our
attention to this connection brings us peace and a sense of
well-being. It brings richer meaning now to our lives in
midlife than we have ever known before.

*My spiritual connection already exists. I only need to
be willing to receive this knowledge for it to be mine.*

Menarche

Women speak of not remembering menarche, this landmark event in their lives, of mothers being secretive about their daughters' first blood, of fathers being embarrassed and turning away, not wanting to know. What possibilities could there be for the development of the mature woman out of such barren ground?

VIRGINIA BEANE RUTTER

Powerful moments denied often become taboo. We have all heard or told horror stories of menarche: the girl of thirteen standing quietly amazed in the bathroom with her new discovery of her own blood, escaping without the presence of injury. Then her mother appears to teach her about menstruation, quite possibly with stern predictions: "You are stuck with this for a good part of your life. They call it 'the curse.' You'll have pains in your belly, and you'll smell bad and be bloody."

Let us hail this event as one that introduces girls to the unique powers of the feminine; let us begin to treat it with respect. Let us become the guardians of the truth of women's bodies for our daughters.

Regardless of how menstruation was presented to me, I can release any negative attitudes and look at it as a positive experience.

Truth

The Truth must dazzle
gradually
Or every man be blind.

EMILY DICKINSON

The older we grow the more we know that truth is always unfolding itself before us and within us. Denial cordons off certain areas where we have not yet reached the truth. Though we sometimes curse denial, it gives us time to concentrate on becoming more honest about one thing at a time.

We would be metaphorically blinded or overwhelmed if we were to see all at once. By midlife we recognize the process more: the exasperation of resistance, the hope that comes with each new layer of truth, the spacious feeling of homecoming we have each time we own an aspect of ourselves more fully. We can cease trying to speed up our revelations and appreciate the rhythm and flow with which they are given.

I locate myself in the truth as I can see it today.

Giving

What do we live for, if it
is not to make life less
difficult for each other?

GEORGE ELIOT

Life is a constant ebb and flow of offerings given and offerings received. We
help others. Others help us. In childhood and youth we are more dependent
and may come to expect that we are to be on the receiving
end. But as we advance in age, it becomes natural to give back
what we have been given.

Sometimes in close relationships we begin to believe we
should be able to get back exactly what we put in. "Fair's fair,"
after all. But giving ceases to be giving when it is motivated
by the desire to exact a gift. Over time we learn to trust that
our generosity will always be rewarded. We do not know how
or when. Perhaps it will simply be the feeling we know in our
heart, that we have grown enough to give back something to
the universe.

*Today, I appreciate the help I have received from
others by offering to help another.*

Perspective

I don't feel archaic but I look at youth today and I often say to myself that I don't know what it is they're after.

BEVERLY

Remember when we were smug teenagers or young adults feeling as if our generation had a handle on the world, had evolved further than our parents. We were hip, carefree, and, depending on our attitudes, had the goods on fun, or purpose, or ambition. If our parents were baffled, all the better. We felt that we had achieved a division from them.

Many of us in midlife are surprised to find ourselves thinking the same thoughts our parents voiced. What does it mean? we wonder. Have we failed to flow with the times? Or is it another way our perspective awaken us to the passage of time? If our parents once said to us, "We used to walk three miles each way to school and back," we can say to our children and grandchildren, "We used to learn math by totaling up long columns of figures in our heads, without calculators or computers."

With age we become more fixed in a moral and political stance that has developed over time. We can take a curious approach toward youth without it being a threat to our own perspective.

Today, I appreciate the differences in the youth culture from mine.

Growing Up

There have always been women who ignored the eternal-youth bandwagon and agreed to grow up, who negotiated the climacteric with a degree of independence and dignity and changed their lives to give their new adulthood space to function and flower.

GERMAINE GREER

It is a challenge for middle-aged women to grow to full maturity when we are barraged with messages to remain youthful and not ourselves. When our mothers were middle-aged, they were still routinely referred to as girls, occasionally as ladies, rarely as women. We in the women's movement of the seventies addressed this with vigor, knowing that a woman who was called a "girl" was not being invited to come into herself completely.

Menopause represents a change from being potent in one's body with the potential of motherhood to a state of being potent with a deepening sense of self and awareness of mortality. It is a time for us to recognize we hold the power to structure our lives the way we want them. It is a time to make the choices that benefit and satisfy us. We settle into ourselves, much like our grandmother might have settled into her very particular rocking chair, and open to a sense of our deeper purpose in being here on the planet.

I allow myself to grow up with dignity and grace.

Self-focus

Now it is my own life I
must acknowledge.

SUSAN GRIFFIN

Many of us who have been busy child-rearing or serving others have an opportunity in midlife to turn to ourselves. If we are uncomfortable with this focus, it may take some practice and discipline for us to grow more at ease in the spotlight, to relax enough to take a good look at ourselves.

Are we bereft because our children have left home? Do we feel as if our primary purpose has already been served and the richness of our life is over? Perhaps we need to mourn this loss, for a rich vein lies before us to be mined. There are facets of ourselves yet to be discovered and many purposes to be served. One of these may be to find our way to the peace in our being.

I bathe in the spotlight of my own vision.

Maturity

Perhaps there is so much mourning over lost youth because we don't have an ethos that makes maturity an asset.

K.

Adolescence is often so painful that it is good we have our approaching adulthood to look forward to as the reward for our survival. But in our culture today, the adulthood that is glorified is a youthful one. Although many of us experience our lives as getting better with each passing year, we also become aware of the incongruity between our experiences and the image our culture presents of us. We are bombarded with messages that youths are more valued than older folks. When we lose our jobs, we have difficulty competing with our younger counterparts, despite our great wealth of experience. When we lose our loves, we are seen as ineligible for new love, though by now we have ripened to a state in which we have learned to love more truly.

Let us visualize a world in which maturity is considered an asset. This more mature society might be less interested in conquest and less pedantic. It might be more balanced, peaceful, and creative.

Today, I recognize and offer my maturity as an asset.

Courage

One of the marks of a
gift is to have the
courage of it.

**KATHERINE ANNE
PORTER**

We all have gifts. Some of us are able
to receive them better than others. This
is always a process that demands
courage of us.

As we grow into midlife, if we have
not accepted and used our gifts, we may feel glum and useless. For, after all, somewhere deep inside, we are going
against the grain of our purpose in being here. Our glumness
helps us to slow down, even stop still, until we are hit on the
head with this awareness and awaken to whatever we are
missing.

Once we have awareness of a gift and are willing to use it,
we may still have fear. But by letting others teach us, by seeking the support we need and having faith in the guidance of
our higher selves, we find the courage to move despite fear.

*I seek the necessary guidance to fully develop
my gifts.*

Sacrifice

Anything of value is
going to cost you
something.

TONI CADE BAMBARA

We cannot pursue one area of life, such
as the development of a new intimate
relationship, or a commitment to working full steam on our art, or making a
major career change or geographical move, without having to
sacrifice our attention to some other area. The acceptance of
sacrifice as a natural part of life is one of the hallmarks of maturity.

As children we have the impression that everything is
meant for us. We are ever awakening from this innocent view
as we are told, yes, this, but no, not that. It seems as if the nos
come from others, not from within us. Later, as adults ourselves, we realize we are dealing not with parents but with the
laws of Nature.

By midlife this reality no longer seems depriving or tragic
if we have grown to accept it. If we have chosen one committed partner, we cannot choose another without losing the
first one. To have a fruitful creative life, we sometimes may
have to forgo a more outgoing social life. If we accept our
choices, the satisfaction with them supplants the cost of
them.

Today, I accept the costs of my choices.

Collective Memory

The old ways of speaking aren't gone. They've changed, of course. There has always been change; there are always new ways to remember.

PAULA GUNN ALLEN

Paula Gunn Allen is referring to changes in the storytelling of Native American women. But this is also true of women telling tales of menopause and aging. Until only recently, The Change has been publicly described only through the eyes and definitions of the medical establishment. The terms and phrases used to describe menopause, such as "deficient in estrogen," have implied that this normal phenomenon is actually a diseased or abnormal state.

Women continue to compare experiences over the kitchen table. And now that we have begun to speak of our knowledge more openly and see our views appear in print more regularly, we intuitively know that older knowledge is there for the seeking. Our matriarchal forebears knew no shame about aging. We can remember them and be fortified by their wisdom as we translate it into our contemporary world.

I listen closely to the voices of the past that reside in the collective unconscious.

Wholeness

Wrinkles here and there
seem unimportant
compared to the *Gestalt*
of the whole person
I have become in this
past year.

MAY SARTON

When we become lost in the mirror, scrutinizing the changing elasticity of our skin, comparing ourselves to the earlier reflection we desire to see, we will do well to refocus our minds on the bigger picture, the gestalt of who we have become. So much of our attitude depends upon the lens we look through. If we look from the depth of our being, we can recognize the many dimensions that are now part of us.

When we appreciate the sum of our dimensions, we find wisdom and freedom from our culture's reflections of us. We have ranged and searched and earned our current ability to come into ourselves. Now we feel more solid than we ever have before. And the seasoning of our experience enriches us as seasoning flavors a soup. Let us take joy in our fullness.

I appreciate the whole of who I am becoming.

Denial

> I have the sensation of standing outside my body and scolding. "What's the matter with you—why don't you *act* the way I feel anymore?"
>
> **GAIL SHEEHY**

"Why don't you act the way I feel" is a familiar experience to us perimenopausal women. We may notice a change in general energy, a diminishing of sexual energy, a creeping in of the blues for no known reason, a jolt of charges in the brain creating flushes, spacing out, or loss of memory. These are all normal responses for a woman whose levels of estrogen are changing. Yet after relying for many years on a certain level of energy, it is difficult for us to believe such basic things can be changing.

We may go along for a while thinking, "This is not the real me." But this *is* real, and nothing takes the spark out of life more than waiting for tomorrow or next year instead of living in this day and this year. Our bodies deserve acceptance. They have served us all these years. Wishing them to be more like they were in younger years will not excuse us from our hot flashes or our feelings of fatigue. Embracing them will make us whole and loving, regardless of the bumps and strains of transit.

I make a practice today of accepting my body exactly as it is.

Choice

Which life should one
lead—the life one likes.
I like writing. I like
change. I like to toss my
mind up and watch to
see where it'll fall.

VIRGINIA WOOLF

Do we like the lives we are leading? Do
we spend our time wishing we were
living someone else's life? Do we know
what we like? Do we know what expresses our nature?

In youth we often don't know.
And so we often travel, not only to different countries but
to the reaches of our hearts and minds. Some of us at
midlife still feel like the eternal traveler. We are changing
careers again. We are ambivalent about where we live. We
want to get up and go again, but we know we will take our
restlessness with us.

Perhaps the best way we can settle into our lives is to
focus on leading the life we like. If we are waiting for another
day to move into that life, this is the time to stop waiting and
go ahead and live it. We have many choices, and no one is
stopping us from making them.

Today, I choose the life I like and go ahead and live it.

Age-passing

Age passing—passing for young enough—is part of all female experience. The foundation of lies built into passing and the fear and loathing of female aging keep the generations of women— decade by decade— divided from each other.

BABA COOPER

We learn a great deal through our thirties and forties about who we are and what really matters to us, and this allows us to assert ourselves more solidly and strongly as we grow older. Yet at the same time that we grow in frankness, ageism encourages us to pass for younger than we are.

We have earned our wisdom by seeking a conscious life through our earlier years. We do not need to accept false stereotypes of older women. These stereotypes, such as the Wicked Witch, the Old Bitch, or the Little Old Lady, either scapegoat or diminish women's integrity and wisdom. We seek to applaud women's integrity and wisdom.

Aging is the natural course of the maturation of life. I reject images that give it a negative connotation.

Aging

but age dries my flesh
with a thousand
wrinkles . . .

SAPPHO

Why is it so hard to embrace our wrinkled skin? We look in the mirror still seeking the more youthful version of ourselves. Often we reject and turn away from our wrinkles, or we moisturize them one more time with the hope that they will cease deepening. Perhaps we see our mother's face in the mirror, or we see our hands turning into the hands of our grandmothers. Mostly we meet this change with dread. Rarely do we welcome it.

Inevitably by around fifty, we see little sags where we had none before. Wrinkles and puckers appear. Especially if we worshiped our youthful body, it is difficult for us to accept these changes.

Why not look upon our wrinkles and emerging sags as well-earned decorations? Why not see within each line the timeline of our wisdom, which we have garnered by surviving? Why not admire our wrinkles as signifying our ever-developing character? When we see a person who has lived to be a hundred and whose face is deeply etched with time, we admire them. Why not admire the earlier version of this at fifty?

*I study and embrace my wrinkles today as signs of
my growing wisdom.*

Productivity

Well, curiously, I seem to have been more prolific in these years. I'm 83. At this point it seemed extremely unlikely that this would happen. It has happened, and I think that I've had to simplify life in order to have it happen.

JOSEPHINE JACOBSEN

One of the reasons we fear aging is because we anticipate a loss of productivity. We can be inspired by someone like poet Josephine Jacobsen, who found herself increasingly prolific in later years. She makes us wonder how much the mind-set of closing up shop creates the reality.

As our energy changes we can ill afford trying to be in all places at once. Rather than regret this, we can focus on the benefits of becoming more discriminating, aligning ourselves in greater harmony with our priorities. The trial and error of our youth can help us to determine what is important now. We know more; we do not need to experiment as much. Instead we can settle into those activities and directions that satisfy us deeply.

I will clarify my focus today and let myself do first the things that give me pleasure and satisfaction.

Quiet Time

A quiet hour is worth
more than anything you
can do in it.

SARAH ORNE JEWETT

We live in a world that provides more validation for doing than for being. For most of us it is easier to believe we are worthy people when we are outwardly productive—going to work, cleaning our houses, raising our children, creating our artwork, checking off items on our endless lists of things to do.

But we are human beings, not human doings. And the nourishment of our soul requires respect for time spent with ourselves or with others in a state of doing nothing—or what appears to be doing nothing but is actually quite something. For it is when we are open to our being that we make conscious contact with a sense of our higher selves and become receptive to a guidance deep within.

Some of us feel so guilty about indulging in this sort of time that our bodies have to break down before it's okay to excuse ourselves from the busy world. But we do not need to wait until we get sick. Especially now as we enter menopause and desire to know our spiritual selves more intimately, let us choose consciously to give ourselves this sort of time.

*Today, I value a quiet hour, or even a portion of an
hour, and I do not seek to fill it but allow
myself to be in it.*

Acceptance of Death

An absolute condition of all successful living, whether for an individual or a nation, is the acceptance of death.

FREYA STARK

A woman's body with its natural changes—manifested first in adolescence by the onset of the menses, then after years of cyclical months by the ending of the menses—comes to know loss on a visceral level. We grieve our loss of the old way as we come into this new age of being older women.

Our ovaries gradually diminish until they are completely gone. We go through the heat of our Change. We let youth die. We become young Crones.

In a culture in which death is embraced as the edge that makes life meaningful by reminding us of our mortality, women on the other side of menopause may be singularly best qualified to acknowledge and integrate a sense of mortality into our daily being. This perspective gives our lives strong meaning and motivates us to fulfill our purpose here on earth.

I do not need to fear death. I recognize it as the most profound passage of all.

Creativity

I had to learn response,
to trust this possibility
for fruition that had not
been before.

TILLIE OLSEN

We are all born with a creative spirit. Some of us see ourselves linked to a greater creative spirit. Yet to express our creativity, we must allow it to gestate and trust that what does emerge is the bearing of our fruit.

As women, our creative nature is often thwarted in its attempt to bear fruit by the demands of children and family, of carrying out the daily chores of life, which are more often tended to by women than by men. Yet for many of us who have raised children, our midlife change may include taking back more energy for ourselves.

When we are able to open ourselves to the time and freedom to creatively express ourselves, we may fear finding nothing, facing a blank page, an untouched canvas, a stage on which we are lost. We have to learn to hold to our quiet, listening for that voice which has gone unheard so often that it may be reluctant to speak.

Today, I will stay quiet long enough to listen.

Wisdom

Living in the white world, people have very strange attitudes about menopausal women. In Indian culture midlife is wisdom. You are a vital woman and there's beauty in that.

MURIEL MIGUEL

Those of us who are white in America often are led to believe that "our way" is the most civilized, the most developed, in short, the *best* way. In relation to attitudes about women and aging, "our way" is barbaric. We can look to other cultures for wiser and more respectful visions about aging.

Taking an honest look at ourselves, we know we have acquired wisdom. We know it is right that we should share this with younger people, mentoring them, offering them the protective shield of our knowledge. Let us bring this knowledge to our culture, regardless of its contrary attitudes. And let us study others' ways not so much to appropriate them as to understand how ours have gone astray.

Today, I will own the wisdom of my midlife.

Memories

> I think, perhaps, one should take a brief look [at those memories one dislikes] and say: "Yes this *is* part of my life but it's done with. It is a strand in the tapestry of my existence."
>
> **AGATHA CHRISTIE**

Many of us who seek to be in the present are beleaguered by our past. We devote much energy to excavating and examining old traumas in order to release them, so that they can become what they should be—memories.

By midlife, we have a more urgent desire than ever to be living in the present. If we haven't already done this work, we are motivated to do it with full attention so that we can move beyond it. As we do, we find the perspective to integrate our past, to make it a strand in our tapestry. There it is not forgotten, but neither is it taking up space in the domain of our present.

I visualize placing my memories into a tapestry of my existence.

Elements

Your body, composed three-quarters of water plus a few terrestrial minerals, a small handful. And this great flame within you, whose nature you do not comprehend.

MARGUERITE YOURCENAR

We usually think of our bodies as very discrete and distinct entities. When they begin to go through The Change, it is difficult not to think something is wrong. We feel a bit of indignation at the betrayal of our bodies. How dare they change on us?

To realize we are made up predominantly of water may help us to flow with the evolution of our changes. And this great flame—what is it? This is our life force, our passion, which leads us magnetically toward people and places where we can meet ourselves more wholly. During menopause this flame may turn into a hot flash, which jolts us and soaks us and passes like a storm. Regardless, it is all part of nature, and we will feel more at ease if we allow the universe to be our cradle.

I visualize the ocean and myself lying beside it. We are not all that different.

Cultural Context

Roughly thirty years ago, when our mothers were being told that the "empty nest syndrome" could cause psychological problems at menopause, Dr. Robert Wilson wrote his best-seller, *Feminine Forever,* in which he asserted that, with HRT [Hormone Replacement Therapy], "Menopause is curable.... Menopause is completely preventable.... Instead of being condemned to witness the death of their own womanhood ... [women] will remain fully feminine—physically and emotionally—for as long as they live."

JOY WEBSTER BARBRE

Menopause is a normal biological phenomenon that every woman who lives long enough will encounter. We are deeply influenced by the prevailing attitudes of the culture around us. Given these attitudes at the time of our mothers' experience with The Change, no wonder we picked up notions—often unspoken—of dread.

We have made some progress, and thankfully, *Feminine Forever* would not be a best-seller today. Still it is important to recognize the recent history that has affected our attitudes. Imagine being told today that our womanhood is dying, when in fact we sense a new mature womanhood about to bloom? We must each make a decision regarding Hormone Replacement Therapy, but regardless of our choice, we know that a hormone will not create or destroy us as women.

I recognize the past but plant myself in the present.

Birth

I've been remembering how we are all so forgiving of pregnancy (little foot kicking my liver) because of the anticipated birth of a child. . . . Can we be as forgiving of meno-pause, giving birth to ourselves?

L.

Do we consider menopause a nuisance and a burden? Do we take a negative attitude, wishing and waiting only for it to be over so it will not bother us anymore? How do our feelings about this attitude change if we anticipate a birth at the end of this passage? If this notion is unbelievable to us, why is that so? Have we been too bombarded with messages that say it is a death to believe the contrary?

We have learned by now that all growth is accompanied by growing pains. It is often pain or discomfort that pushes us to take the time to reexamine what is occurring in our lives, without or within. Menopause presents us with an extended time full of reminders, such as hot flashes, to feel ourselves potent and heated with change. During this time we renew our commitment to ourselves for the next phase. We open ourselves to expressing the parts that have been dormant. We integrate our past as preparation to live in the present.

I forgive the discomforts of menopause as it prepares me for a birth.

Fear of Aging

... it takes so much effort to hold on to the illusion of youth, to keep the fear of age at bay, that in doing so we could fail to recognize the new qualities and strengths that might emerge.

BETTY FRIEDAN

Are we afraid of aging? Do we even know we are afraid? Why would we not be afraid? Many of us with aging parents see the quandaries they face—the loss of sturdy health and independence. Many no longer have an extended family to rely on, and caretaking institutions leave much to be desired. Isn't it enough to watch their struggle, without realizing that we, too, are advancing in age and will eventually be just as frail?

We focus on attempts to retain our youth rather than actively and creatively developing options for our future. If we concentrate instead on taking a fresh and open look at aging, we will discover the new strengths of our elders. We will begin to pay attention to them as models and see what they have that we may wish to emulate.

Looking beyond my fear of aging today, I see my elders more fully.

Broadening

I have been able, as I grow older, to extend my range of fellow-feeling: to animals, for instance, to nations, even to inanimate objects. . . . I do not feel in the least foolish in apologizing to a table, if I trip over its leg, or jollying along a recalcitrant automobile with encouraging words.

JAN MORRIS

While the prevailing notion insists that people narrow with age, if we listen to individuals logging in their experience, we discover the many ways in which we broaden. Many of us become more attuned to nature. We are able not only to bear silence and stillness but to love it, and in so doing we hear the musical sounds of birds and wind and running water. We might have heard them once as children and then lost their sounds to the bustle of an ambitious life.

The more we attend to the life in every being and object around us, the more we revere our selves. A tree simply exists and continues to grow upward. It witnesses its neighbors and houses certain animals. It usually lives a long life, but eventually it dies. By attuning ourselves to it, we can feel our stalwart self. We can feel how we are rooted in the earth, the Great Mother.

I allow myself the freedom to commune with animals, plants, or inanimate objects around me.

Receiving

All we need is already ours if we believe it to be so. Our challenge is being open to receive it and gracious enough to appreciate it.

HELENE LERNER-ROBBINS

So much of craving comes from a distortion of perspective. We fear we do not have enough. Yet the only way to have enough is to know that what we already have is enough. Most of the time we do not know this because we are busy seeking more.

Midlife slows us down a bit and helps us to redirect our vision so that we can see what we do have and receive it with gratitude. Do we have the basic necessities of food, clothing, shelter? Do we have loving friends and family. Do we have our health? A sense of community? Hope and vision? Are our hearts open? Do we have a sense of well-being? How can we be satisfied by these elements of our lives if we do not stop and notice them?

I am grateful today for the provisions of my life.

Separation

Birth is, I think, an attenuated process. . . . Each phase of the process involves separation, which may or may not be physical but always carries heavy psychic freight.

NANCY MAIRS

Surely the onset of menses is one of our births. It marks the beginning of our separation from childhood. Menopause is yet another birth, a second coming of age into maturity. It marks the final stage of our separation from youth.

Separation arouses our fears of not having or being enough. We are faced with the fact that we may not have accomplished or become all that we ideally imagined by this time.

The pain of separation often has to do with unfinished business. If we simply take the time to attend to what is unfinished now, we may very well be able to move on with ease.

I am grateful for each new birth that comes my way.

Time

The life of sensation is
the life of greed; it
requires more and more.
The life of the spirit
requires less and less;
time is ample and its
passage sweet.

ANNIE DILLARD

Time is both objective and subjective. It
seems to slow down when we are full
and speed up when we are hungry.
When we are obsessive we spin through
time with the feeling we are losing it, as,
indeed, in a sense we are. For our energy
is circular and does not advance us.

As we go through menopause, we may find ourselves
wishing to stop time, to revert back to our younger selves.
When we are afflicted with this urge, we do well to turn to
our spiritual connection and let ourselves appreciate being
who we are. We are all of us spirits in residency in these bodies, which tell us of the passage of time.

*When I want more and more, I turn inward to my
spirit and receive the love that enfolds me
and has no limits.*

Wisdom

In the early matriarchal community, menstrual blood was a source of wonder. When the "blood of life" no longer flowed regularly from the body of an aging woman, it was assumed to be held inside her for a grand purpose.

JACQUELYN H.
GENTRY AND
FAYE M. SEIFERT

The old knowledge of the early matriarchal communities seems still to reside in us, so these old myths, at least as metaphors, ring true. Did we not have a great sense of wonder at our first menstrual blood? And did it not always contain for us the mystery of the workings of the body? Even a thorough understanding of anatomy and physiology does not diminish the body's mystery, in both its regularities and its irregularities.

Crones in the old days had the magnitude of wisdom, the wisdom to see life in its fullest dimensions. They were attuned to the cyclical aspects of Nature, its transformational quality. Always life is leading toward death; always death is leading toward birth. To live with this knowledge is to appreciate becoming.

I embrace the cyclical nature of my life and enjoy my wisdom.

Weight

I used to be able to eat just about anything I wanted to. Now whatever I imbibe seems to go so directly to my waist. I feel as if I hardly get to taste it on the way down.

IRENE

Some of the changes that go with midlife require a reacquaintance with our bodies, these bodies we have come to rely upon as so familiar. Many women find that fighting the "middle-aged spread" is like having an argument with Nature.

There is evidence to support the fact that weightier women have less difficulty with menopause—less severe hot flashes and fewer problems with osteoporosis, since estrogen is made in fat cells.

So perhaps Mother Nature does want us to spread a little.

Susun S. Weed suggests a slow weight gain of a pound a year from forty to fifty to support the most intense part of menopause. Regular exercise can be balanced with weight gain to ensure distribution between fat and muscle.

I determine the best weight for me for my menopausal journey.

Awareness

For our lives. How long will they be? Can we count on another 20 years? I shall be fifty on 25th, Monday . . . & sometimes feel that I have lived 250 years already, & sometimes that I am still the youngest person in the omnibus.

VIRGINIA WOOLF

Our perceptions about our age and our wisdom fluctuate widely. Approaching fifty, we become conscious that a certain weighty stack of years has accumulated behind us. Where were we? Did we miss some of it? Because surely it feels too soon for us to be fifty. On the other hand, there are ways in which we are weary, and at least our age confirms that we have been around for a while.

What can we count on? Virginia Woolf did not have another twenty years as she wondered to her diary, though she imagined the fine reading she would do if she were to have them. It is good to become aware that our time here is finite. If we are afraid of death, this awareness presents an opportunity to face our fear. If we are not afraid of death, we are free to use our sense of the limits of our life span to order our priorities so that we become more fully ourselves.

I center myself through awareness of my age.

Creativity

I notice that it is only when my mother is working in her flowers that she is radiant almost to the point of being invisible—except as Creator: hand and eye. She is involved in work her soul must have. Ordering the universe in the image of her personal conception of Beauty.

ALICE WALKER

Creativity is not something that wanes as the body becomes less physically active. Rather, it is an energy that feeds the soul and, conversely, that springs forth when the soul is being attended to.

The time of our Change is an ideal time to allow our creativity to flourish. This can take many forms. For some of us, it will be expression—allowing ourselves to write, paint, draw, garden, act, make music. For some of us, it will be reception—allowing through an open door our desire for deeper understanding.

Today, I allow myself to see my personal conception of Beauty, of Truth, represented in the universe.

Acceptance

Whence come I and on
what wings that it
should take me so long,
humiliated and exiled, to
accept that I am myself?

COLETTE

Have we been exiled from ourselves?
Have we been performing from a script
rather than from our own deepest urg-
ings? Have we feared that if we were
simply ourselves, we would reveal some
deficit, some failure to be worthy?

Accepting ourselves is a lifelong process. By midlife most
of us are getting a good taste of it. Things we might have once
thought to change about ourselves we realize we only need to
love—our foibles and vulnerabilities, our quirks and domestic
customs. Even some of the ways in which we are like our
mothers . . . or our fathers.

We grow up hearing many contrary messages. *Be like me.
Be superwoman if you want to count as good as a man. Be perfect.*
If we have tortured ourselves with these notions, we can give
them up now and feel the joy of simply being ourselves.

I fit in my skin today, accepting myself for who I am.

Forgiveness

Forgiveness—essential to any healing process—is . . . a central part of the creative process, for in order to create we must continually forgive ourselves for our inability to embody the perfect vision; we must forgive ourselves for our finitude.

LINDA SCHIERSE LEONARD

We become increasingly aware of our finitude in midlife. And with this awareness we may panic that we will not get "enough" done in our lifetime. We are discouraged by our imperfections and the ways we feel as if life has failed us. But how often do we think about the healing power of forgiveness?

When we do forgive ourselves for our limits and imperfections, we are acknowledging our humanity. In response we receive the flow of our creative energy. We step out of our own light and see how light comes through us. Our creations may be art forms, or new ideas for programs, or forums with which to share what we have learned with the world. They may be newer, more subtle ways to reach and communicate with others. In finding the creator within us, we find ourselves bound to all creation.

Today, I willingly forgive my own limits and allow the infinity of creative energy to flow through me.

The Unknown

I am committed to the Tantric path on the journey which takes us through the deep, dark, unknown places in life, into the light of self-realization. In the Tantric tradition, Shiva and Shakti represent the male and female, seeking wholeness through this union.

SHAKTI GAWAIN

Midlife is a time for many of us to journey to some of the darker, unknown places within us. We do this to deepen into a rich, mature adulthood. We do this to discover the wealth we have within, which then expands our vision so that we are able to see the same wealth in others.

At times we must wander in the wilderness a while before we begin to recognize the figures that are within us. For instance, some of us may have trouble locating our masculine energy, while others have trouble locating the feminine. But ultimately, we each have both masculine and feminine energies within ourselves to develop and bring to union. Let us not concern ourselves with how close we are to union. The fact that we are on the path is worthy of our greatest respect.

I am pioneering my own unknown territory.

Containment

During pregnancy a woman finds herself in a deep state of inner-containment while creation and transformation take place in her womb. Emergence comes when the blood flows in childbirth and the baby is born. . . . Later in life, when her blood ceases, she returns to another state of self-containment.

VIRGINIA BEANE RUTTER

Menopause is a passage into the self-containment that will allow us to remember parts of ourselves and ripen with the wisdom of our years. Our containment does not keep us from sharing our lives with others; it sparks a creative dialogue between our inner and outer lives that can be a source of great vitality.

As women we have been trained to be more available to others than to ourselves. Thus containment may at first feel alien or selfish. Yet in menopause, as in pregnancy, our bodies take the lead and create this state for us. We need only accept their natural rhythm and direction. When our bloods cease we intuitively know we have more held within us to attend to.

I embrace myself today in the knowledge that my body contains my full life force.

Journey to the Mountain

My help is in the
mountain
That I take away with
me.

NANCY WOOD

Moses journeyed to the mountain. The Greeks traveled to the oracle on the mountainside at Delphi. Why is the mountain the place to crystallize change? And why do we need to do that now?

Symbolically, going to the mountain is a way to achieve height, a look at the long view, a full perspective. At midlife we are often caught up trying to squeeze vitality out of old habits or once-lively pursuits that no longer satisfy us. We need to step out of our ordinary lives and take a look at the long view to see what we desire and what we can begin to change.

The mountain offers us a foundation of stone. We are grounded by this stone as we listen carefully and receive direction. We let go of our desire to fall back into the old and prepare ourselves to move onward in our journey.

I seek a place from which I can see the long view.

Grief

I was surrounded by friends, but when somebody dies, you're completely alone. Nobody can die for you; you've got to die for yourself. And in that moment you feel the vacuum. It's a total vacuum and nobody can enter that space.

JUDITH JAMISON

Many of us lose one or both of our parents, or someone who has been a significant presence in our lives, at the time of our midlife. If we have not dealt with the death of someone close before, we may find ourselves baffled.

We find ourselves alone, bereft, perhaps inconsolable. At first it is difficult to believe our mother or our father could actually be gone. Their death brings us face to face with our own mortality. The fact that they are gone puts us closer to our own limits.

Though others offer consolation, no one else experiences exactly what we are going through. We are left to grapple with the loss as well as the loneliness inside us. We do not need to be ashamed of this feeling. We can simply allow it to exist without resistance and know that eventually it will pass with time.

*The ground shifts under my feet when a parent dies.
I stay present through what follows and know
that I am fine.*

Rituals

Menopause rituals have altogether disappeared from our intensely patriarchal society. Yet in antiquity there were rites of passage from the Mother to the Crone stage of women's life, especially for the elder priestesses and clan mothers who became the magistrates, healers, and oracles of their groups.

BARBARA G. WALKER

With the loss of menopausal rituals and of the consecration of priestesses and oracles, we lost part of our story, as if a strong thread affirming our inner reality had unraveled. We lost the figures who made it their job to guide women through their life stages, beginning with a girl's transition through menarche.

Today we see the reemergence of priestesses and healers—women who bring others together, conduct rituals, and share their spiritual understanding of these passages. These women are reviving ancient memories that seem to reside in all of us. They show us how to tap the old power and knowledge women held in antiquity, instead of letting it remain lost.

Today, I let the old knowledge reside in me and guide me.

Fear

Research shows that premenopausal women have a much more negative view of menopause than women who have gone through it. Women who have experienced menopause discover there is nothing to fear.

LONNIE BARBACH,
PH.D.

We always have more fear about that of which we are ignorant. We want to know, before we encounter an experience, just what its parameters are. We want to know what to expect. But with many aspects of life we cannot achieve this sort of control. We must settle for dropping our expectations and adopt a willingness to explore and appreciate the adventure as it unfolds.

Do women after menopause have a more positive view than women facing it simply because they are on the other side? Or do they know something those of us who are only entering it don't know? As more women break the silence and speak of their experiences, we begin to form a new picture, one that has a positive side that balances the scale, one that can even excite and entice us.

I recognize my fear casts a shadow on new experiences.

Healing

The cure for anything is salt water—sweat, tears, or the sea.

ISAK DINESEN

Menopause must be walked through a day at a time just like any other life event. Along the way are cumbersome problems: layers of clothing that have to be removed with hot flashes, moods that rock sanity, dry skin, shrinking bones.

This is a passage that brings forth regret and grieving: Why did I not do more that I wanted to in youth? How is it possible this middle age crept up on me while I wasn't looking? Will I ever get to be who I want to be before it is all over?

Tears always heal us. So does labor. And the sea embraces and buoys us. We look upon her great mass and power with wonder and awe. We look upon our great problems and are reminded not to fight the forces of Nature but to give in and float through our passage.

I let salt water buoy me on my journey.

Change

Time is a dressmaker specializing in alterations.

FAITH BALDWIN

So much changes over time, sometimes dramatically, but more often so gradually that we hardly notice alterations have been made until we wake up one morning and notice that we have been refitted.

What fits us at one age does not fit us at another. This is a natural progression of events, though it is not always easy to see because we live in a culture bent on glorifying youth and giving little visibility to those of us in more mature ages.

The vitality of our lives comes with being in the now. It comes with staying present as we are changing. We step out into unknown territory, dressed in old clothes. We realize our coat is too heavy and our shoes pinch; nothings fits right. Gently we snip away and let the pieces fall in a trail behind us.

I make the necessary alterations to fit my growth.

Success

Success makes you ridiculous; you end up wearing nightgowns to dinner.

NATALIE GOLDBERG

What is success? The very word conjures up awards presentations, those pinnacle moments when we are singled out from others. We all have fantasies of being prizewinners, of making it to the top, but these fleeting moments, even if they do happen to us, are only symbolic markers of our day-to-day journey.

Perhaps more heroic than any single adventure or achievement is our daily devotion to turning the ordinary wheels of life. The getting up and going to work one more day when we are weary. The patience and perseverance to stand up for ourselves one more time in that disagreement we've had so many times before with our partner. The plodding work we do to learn the road map of our inner selves.

Our success with these ventures rarely gets lauded with trophies. We settle for an occasional warm glow in our hearts.

Today, I count my quieter successes.

Listening

Women tell time by the body. They are like ducks. They are always fastened to the earth, listening for its small animal noises.

ANNE SEXTON

At menarche our bodies clearly tell us a new stage of life is approaching. While we may still feel like little girls, our bodies are sprouting breasts and pubic hair. We listen for the way to move with this new body.

From time to time, up till around forty, we hear our body's urge to have babies. Some of us have them; some of us do not. Those of us who do not have babies hear our bodies speaking louder as we near the age when bearing children becomes riskier. We may go through great conflict and regret, even if it has been our choice to remain childless.

At menopause we again listen to our bodies. They guide us once more into a new stage of life. They show us that we have lived long enough to acquire some sags and wrinkles—and also wisdom.

I listen to the guidance of my body.

Heritage

Paraclesus said that witches taught him everything he knew about healing. I am seeking, in the myths and symbols which are my inheritance, an affirmation of those mysterious qualities which have somehow become downgraded and made risible as "old wives' tales" and "female intuition."

ALLEGRA TAYLOR

We are now discovering and claiming our inheritance as middle-aged and older women. Witches were healers who upset the world order of patriarchy, so much so that many of them were put to death. It is a measure of their force that they have survived so grandly in our imagination, even through periods when we might have colluded and looked askance at them.

Where would we be without "old wives' tales" and "female intuition"? These are aspects of our wisdom. They offer us the knowledge that we are going to become grand old women, that there is something very special to this passage of midlife, that our own wisdom will both heal us and make us healers.

I embrace my inheritance with open arms.

Foundation

They are like bone, the rocks. They frame. They remain. They hold you.

JUDY GRAHN

Rocks are essential in our lives. They provide a foundation to support us, like our bony skeleton supports our body. Our mother may be our rock, or our father. Our friends may be rocks. We need the people around us to be sturdy and steady and solid as rock.

As we make our midlife transition, rocks remain under our feet to ground us. Change is in the air. Heat rushes through us. We are powerless over our hormones as they adjust to new levels. When we feel passively tossed about by these events, we need more than ever to hold onto our rocks.

How fortunate we are that there is always a rock to be found.

I stand on a fine, strong rock today and notice how nicely it endures against time.

Transitions

When a time of transition comes, if the ego is in charge of an orderly, reflective, conscious process, then the woman considers priorities, loyalties, values, and reality factors. She does not force resolution of conflicting choices; resolution comes after the issues have become clear.

**JEAN SHINODA
BOLEN, M.D.**

By midlife most of us have learned a few times too many that it doesn't pay to force things. When we try that, while we may get what we think we want, we discover it is the wrong thing and not at all what we need. When we try to speed things up by doggedly and willfully pushing ahead, we come to see that we are often detouring from our true course and going nowhere important.

Now we are in a passage. Our body demonstrates with this passage that transitions are not meant to be accomplished overnight. We have an opportunity to see that our emotional and spiritual changes can be related to as an "orderly, reflective, conscious process." We have an opportunity to experience the patience we have developed, which helps us wait for resolution. In the waiting comes the clarity that lets us decide our conflicts with a confidence that gives us peace.

When I don't know what to do, I do nothing. I wait until my direction appears.

Burn Out

How frightening it was to leave space open without rushing to fill up every nook and cranny with familiar distractions. I learned to sit for hours without any plan and without being sure . . . of anything.

HOLLY NEAR

Sometimes we can only slow down enough to make a transition by burning out. We go single-mindedly past our limits, offering ourselves through service to others. We ignore the signals of our bodies when they try to tell us we are worn down and need refueling. When we receive these signals, we may be compelled to push harder than ever, until eventually we are brought still through injury or illness.

Then we must learn to sit still with the windows and doors of our soul open for an airing out. We learn the discipline of releasing distracting thoughts as they enter our mind, not fixating on them. We learn to let the presence of our heart take all the space it wants. This may bring us to tears or joy. So be it. We relent and relax.

Eventually we feel the trickle of energy begin to flow and fill us back up from the bottom of our well.

I nourish my being with quiet, open space and time.

Power

The true representation of power is not of a big man beating a smaller man or a woman. Power is the ability to take one's place in whatever discourse is essential to action and the right to have one's part matter. This is true in the Pentagon, in marriage, in friendship, and in politics.

CAROLYN G. HEILBRUN

We must be able to speak up in order to have our power. If the general discourse about aging does not include a point of view that accurately describes our midlife experience, we need to express it and press for its inclusion.

In our daily lives we need to take our place and have our part matter. We have learned to trivialize or minimize our part. Sometimes we have learned to even sacrifice our part. As midlife women we may feel as if we are losing whatever power we once had, since we are losing that more youthful appearance that women are led to believe is their power.

Our true power comes with gathering in the wealth and range of our experience and holding it within us until it percolates into wisdom.

I take my full place at the table of life today and make my part matter.

Suffering

Knowledge by suffering
entereth,
And life is perfected by
death.

ELIZABETH BARRETT
BROWNING

How much of our innocence would we be willing to give up, if not for suffering? We seem to cling mightily to an idealized, youthful view of life, prizing romance and dreaming of when everything will come around right rather than accepting the bumpy experience that actually presents itself. In our false innocence, we often miss the present—the small but satisfying pleasure of a moment of real connection in a day, the feel of the sun on our face, the smell of a rose.

Much as we dread suffering, it brings us to an understanding of life that grounds us. And from grounding we gain balance, the ability to act less extremely and in greater accord with our needs.

In midlife we come to know that there is no sense in trying to move away from suffering. We will always be faced anew with problems that cause suffering. Our challenge is not to escape them but to face them in such a way as to allow our suffering to reveal our humanity.

I do not suffer needlessly. My suffering enlarges me.

Purpose

> Nothing contributes so much to tranquilize the mind as a steady purpose—a point on which the soul may fix its intellectual eye.
>
> **MARY WOLLSTONECRAFT SHELLEY**

Confusion often comes in midlife because of a loss of steady purpose. Some of us have served long and devotedly in a particular career or job, always before with great interest, and now we discover that our interest has waned. Some of us have been devoted to raising our children, and now they have left home. It is easy to feel lost without this steady sense of purpose.

Our purpose is not lost, only our awareness of it. Our task now is to listen for the direction that will guide us to our next purpose. We are not done; in many ways we are just beginning.

Perhaps our next purpose will be to take an inward journey to know ourselves better before we return to offer service and connection to others. Perhaps we are in preparation for a change of career. Perhaps we will make a commitment to fulfill our creative talents. Whatever our destiny, the journey to seek our purpose has a steadying influence on us.

My purpose stands before me; I seek the vision to see it.

Pain

Pain—has an Element of
    Blank—
It cannot recollect
When it begun—or if
    there were
A time when it was not—

EMILY DICKINSON

We each encounter painful times in our lives. Eventually we understand the flawed memory of pain, though this is not a lesson we learn just once, but again and again. For as soon as we are surrounded by our pain, we think that we will always feel it and nothing else.

But pain does pass. Isn't it odd to think that there will come a time when we will never again feel the pain of menstrual cramps? A few months without them and we will even begin to wonder if we could conjure up the feeling if we wanted to. For it is also in the nature of pain to be forgotten once it has lost its source.

In matters of the heart, pain may leave a longer trace. But in this pain we learn of our wounds, and through our wounds we come to know compassion.

Regardless of how entrenched it feels, all pain passes eventually.

Dark Mother

Most ancient religions made a definite symbolic place for this darker feminine image. It was perceived as present and powerful, in equal proportion to the beautiful, sensual, divine giver of birth, light, love, and nurture—just as night must coexist with day, winter with summer.

BARBARA G. WALKER

Christianity replaced the prepatriarchal Goddess religion, abandoning the notion that the cosmos functioned cyclically. No God or Goddess existed to symbolically contain fear. Rather, people were taught to fear God. While certain feminine energies of the ancient Goddess—the Virgin and the Mother—were assimilated into the worship of Mary in Christianity, the Crone phase—containing the opposites of dark and light, beauty and ugliness—was too threatening and was omitted.

Today we need the Crone, not only for our individual power as we pass into the Crone's age but for our society to come to greater maturity. We must see within ourselves the energies of rejection and abandonment; we must see the failures that lead to wars. We must not deny these energies but learn to integrate them.

I recognize my cyclical nature and the cycles of nature.

Security

No one can build his
security upon the
nobleness of another
person.

WILLA CATHER

On what do we build our security?
Often we attempt to build it upon our
associations with others. If we know an
esteemed person, doesn't that guarantee
that we are esteemed, too? It does not.
That person may act as a mirror for us, reflecting qualities we
respect and admire and would like to develop in ourselves,
but we must do our own work to achieve security.

Security grows with self-knowledge and with a right
sense of our place in the universe. Having the humility to
know when to listen for the guidance of our spirit or higher
self gives us security. For our will, left to run amok, is not
enough to show us where we are going.

*My security comes from within me, from knowing
I am a child of the universe, never entirely dependent
upon my associations with others.*

Love

When we [the middle-aged or old] have the advantage is in loving itself—we know so much more; we are so much better able to handle anxiety, frustration, or even our own romanticism; and deep down we have such a store of tenderness.

MAY SARTON

Age softens skin and bones, gums and the middle of our bodies. It also softens attitudes. It takes us many years to realize that self-righteousness does not make us right, that we have probably been guilty at some time of most of the behaviors that irritate us in others, that we would do best to accept ourselves rather than reject others when they mirror the features we dislike.

Our growing store of tenderness makes us better able to love. While it may be harder to bond with a partner because we each have fully formed lives already, this difficulty is compensated by our seasoned ability to cope with our frustrations when we hit the hard places. We more readily know that this too shall pass. We have learned to hold more feelings in the same moment—love and anger, for instance. We are familiar with our own reactions when threatened. We have come to appreciate how much of loving goes beyond romance, and we are ready to have gratitude for its presence in our lives.

I appreciate my growing ability to love.

Sexuality

> I allow myself much more time to look at my lover's body, to stroke her and caress her. Part of this tenderness comes from my sense of our combined years—almost 90 years of life between us—and thus even time becomes an erotic ally.
>
> **JOAN NESTLE**

Certainly there are changes in the erotic domain during midlife. Women often experience vaginal dryness with some of the hormonal changes of menopause. Yet the more endemic problem is that we hear too often that we are going to dry up like old prunes.

There are simple solutions to the alterations in our vaginal secretions, ranging from external lubricants to herbal options to progesterone cream. And if we pay attention to our true experiences and talk to other women in midlife and older, we can learn to dismiss the old caricature of midlife sexuality. In this way we discover the best-kept secrets.

Many women report that their sexuality blossoms in midlife. We have had time to establish what we like, and we are not afraid to ask for it. We can appreciate our experience and that of our lovers. If we have spent many years with one partner, we can revel in the depth and texture of our knowledge of each other.

I free my midlife sexuality from prescribed notions of what it ought to be.

Analyzing

The moral is . . . never systematize—not until you're 70: & have been supple & sympathetic & creative & tried out all your nerves and scopes.

VIRGINIA WOOLF

We have a tendency to want to organize life into a system, to analyze and explain all that happens, to predict outcomes and try to control them. Once we find or create a system that seems attuned to us, we often try to impose it on others: "Why don't you do it *our way,* the best way?"

Life is not so much complex as mysterious and beyond the limits of our comprehension. Systematizing our thinking always reduces life in such a way as to only skim the richness of its texture. When someone close to us is dying, we may encounter the mystery of how our own life lights up with heightened awareness of its preciousness. Or we may be mystified by the way love opens our hearts and hate closes them.

At midlife we are far too young to surround ourselves with a rigid system. It is a good time to allow empathy to range far and wide and to renew our sense of awe at how little we know.

I step outside of any systems I have created around me and look at the world anew.

Denial

The pursuit of youth was blinding us to the possibilities of age. Could denial of our own aging block further growth, foreclose the emergence of a new life otherwise open to us?

BETTY FRIEDAN

Why do some people seem to blossom as they age while others grow crusty and brittle? Can an attitude of acceptance be the key that makes the difference? Much evidence has been gathered to support this.

We always develop in the areas we attend to, while those areas we neglect atrophy. If we are too frightened to accept the fact of our aging, if, instead, we are holding up a wall of denial, then surely we are unable to imaginatively explore the possibilities our aging offers and envision any new directions.

If all we do is pursue youth harder and faster than ever, we predominantly see our own frustration. If we are lucky, we finally exhaust ourselves and, dropping with fatigue, become defenseless enough to receive a vision of a life that can satisfy our age.

I relax about aging and let in the vision of a new age for me.

Limits

The acceptance of limits, of separateness, of finitude, is clearly itself a central task of menopause. Something *is* over; someday we *will* die. Full coming to terms with our death is probably the task of the far side of this period into which menopause initiates us, not of its beginning.

CHRISTINE DOWNING

If we think of menopause as a slow initiation into the lessons and wisdoms of confronting our mortality, we can appreciate that it is a lengthy process. For we would certainly not be able to raise up this wisdom overnight. Much of us remains in protest: "But I don't want to grow older," "I don't want to accept limits," "I want more," "I haven't yet gotten my due."

If there is a needy child within us still crying out for more, we must attend this aspect to be able to accept limits, seeing these limits not as a punishment of deprivation.

In the deepening midlife journey we learn that there is plenty to have, but we cannot have everything. We must choose. We must prioritize. We must leave some things behind. This is not cause for suffering if we can rejoice in what we have chosen.

Acceptance of my limits without bitterness comes when I make good choices for myself.

Redemption

I think civilizations are lost in groups but they're saved one on one.

LUCILLE CLIFTON

We can look at the history of the decline of civilizations and take a hopeless, hedonistic attitude, or we can focus on our ability to learn with age and history. The only corner of the world we can be absolutely sure of changing is the little piece we are standing on. But if we do our part to change that piece, the effect will make a difference.

Take garbage for instance. In a city we need only walk the streets to see how our contemporary way of living creates mounds of it. Our individual, conscientious efforts to recycle may seem futile in the face of the paper and plastic mountains we see around us. But it is precisely our care that is cause for hope. Our conscientiousness not only cleans up our corner but by its example may inspire others to clean up theirs.

I take seriously my place in contributing to my civilization.

Obsolescence

I can't quite figure out who I am right now other than a forty-four-year-old woman adjusting to a totally new and largely unplanned obsolescence that I am proud of but regret.

NIKKI GIOVANNI

Thus Nikki Giovanni describes her new-found status as a mother whose son, having resided under her roof for eighteen years, has reached his "majority." This is a condition many midlife women find familiar. Because motherhood is such a demanding job of serving others, mothers whose children are leaving home undergo a major life transition.

We understand that retirement from a long-term career demands a profound readjustment. Why would we expect any less when it comes time for a woman to lay her active mothering to rest? We must find ourselves anew without this identification. We must feel our way through obsolescence until it becomes an open space in which we explore those aspects of ourselves that are ready to emerge.

Obsolescence is not a deficit; it is a condition potent with spaciousness and possibility.

Priorities

I used to dread getting older because I thought I would not be able to do all the things I wanted to do, but now that I am older I find that I don't want to do them.

LADY NANCY ASTOR

Think of all the things about which we once said, "I'd like to do this and that, go here and there." Do they all come back to haunt us as we realize the constraints of growing older? No. Rather we notice with interest that many of them never rose to the top of the list, and as we became more centered they actually fell away.

Life has a way of working out its problems. Gradually it dawns on us that much of our worry has been wasted because, while we thought no problem could be solved without our constant obsessive attention, we find that new problems always come along, often changing things so much that old problems mysteriously evaporate.

The natural selection of the sifting and sorting of life helps me know what is important.

Awakening

[In the Sarvodaya Movement] one's personal awakening (*purushodaya*) is integral to the awakening of one's village (*gramodaya*), and both play integral roles in *deshodaya* and *vishvodaya,* the awakening of one's country and one's world.

JOANNA MACY

We are fortunate to live in a time of awakening about menopause, a time in which we are influenced by the awakening of others and one in which we are also playing a part. Our personal awakening reverberates in our community, ultimately reaching beyond our community to our country and our world.

How do we awaken? We listen to our bodies. We educate our minds. We speak with others about their experiences and ours. We pay attention to our feelings. We seek the guidance that we need from others. We receive the wisdom of our higher selves.

We are ever awakening, and through this greater awareness, we shine a light that enables others to see.

I place great value in my awakening.

Giving

The fragrance always remains in the hand that gives the rose.

HEDA BEJAR

In our younger years we don't think too much about giving. Most of us are more concerned with getting. We want to have our independence. We want to "get ahead." We want to get what we think we have coming to us.

By midlife our values develop more roundly. We don't see our energy as directed in a linear way, from point A to point B, but we see the value of the circle. We see how our inner development evolves in a spiral fashion. Quite naturally, we become more concerned with giving.

When we attempt to give but find ourselves keeping score—giving for one-upmanship or to create a debt—we have a chance to learn about the parts of us that are still needy for attention. This, too, is useful, even if we have to recognize that our gift was not a gift but a manipulation. When we are ready, we can give truly and generously, and then we will know the pleasure of the scent that remains.

A gift freely given makes grace tangible.

Grace

When we experience consciousness of the unity in which we are embedded, the sacred whole that is in and around us, we exist in a state of grace. At such moments our consciousness perceives not only our individual self, but also our larger self, the self of the cosmos. The gestalt to unitive existence becomes palpable.

CHARLENE SPRETNAK

Grace is always nearby, yet it's not a quality that responds to manipulation. We cannot make it happen. It is something to be received, not something to be demanded. We can only prepare for it by opening our hearts to all that is around us.

A spiritual practice of any sort may bring us more frequently into the warm light of grace, for through a spiritual practice we demonstrate our willingness to transcend our individual self and align with a broader sense of spirit. We remind ourselves we are a being among beings. We remind ourselves we are whole unto ourselves at the same time that we are connected to all others.

Grace is a gift of the universe always present nearby.

Reverse Adolescence

My genitals have changed. The hair sparser. The outer lips smaller. A friend said, "Menopause is adolescence in reverse. Remember when we got our first pubic hair, when our genitals began to develop . . . ?" In a sense it's like that: adolescence preparing our bodies for the sexual round, the life force throbbing within us. Menopause preparing us for independent strength, friendship with death, wisdom.

SANDY BOUCHER

Doesn't much of aging resemble this hourglass shape? We start out entirely self-focused as babies, and at the very end of our life we have an inner mandate to once again focus our energy much more exclusively on ourselves.

Menopause can be a sort of precursor to this. It directs us to go within and rearrange and resettle ourselves for the second half of life. It shows us through our bodily changes that our purposes may be changing. Then it allows us to open back out into life with gusto and new power, as we did after the passage of the early awkward years of adolescence when we came into our adult selves.

I trust in Mother Nature's rearrangement of my body for a new period of life.

Hot Flashes

The thermostat is off
and I overheat like a
stalled car.

JUDITH BISHOP

Women have a wide variety of experiences with hot flashes during menopause. A small percentage of us never have them at all. Others have them as frequently as every fifteen minutes, repeating on this basis for many months. Some women continue to do whatever they are doing right through them; others feel as if their synapses are jumping and they can't think straight. Some women even learn to use them to their advantage; for example, one woman reported that she waited on cold winter mornings for a hot flash before she got out of bed to dress and stoke her wood stove.

When hot flashes first come, they may feel as if they are signals that something is wrong. We may panic, just as we do when we see steam emanating from under the hood of our car. But they are only a signal that our hormone levels are peaking and ebbing, playing havoc with our body's thermostat. We do not need to stop. Our motor is not going to stall. We can learn to relax as best we can, wipe the sweat from our brow, and continue moving forward.

I envision the heat of my hot flashes as fueling important changes.

The Moon

How often in those years of lying alone Carrie has been annoyed by the uselessness of her cyclic bloodletting. Yet as it wanes now, coming in unexpected clots, sometimes seeping onto her skirts . . . and stopping its flow as suddenly, she feels regret. Life is undeniably waning; but it isn't decay. Surrender maybe. The end of her long marriage to the moon.

CHARLOTTE PAINTER

How often have we felt that our menses were connected to the cycles of the moon? Perhaps the full moon drew our period to begin. Perhaps she charted for us an unconscious awareness of our womb with her inevitable coming to fullness, waxing and waning. She married each of us at menarche.

At menopause she shows us that waning is not decay; it only leads to the next stage in the cycle of life. As Crones we will have a new relationship to the moon. We hold our blood within. We let our wisdom out.

The moon in all her splendor and in her ever-present nature watches me and reminds me to wonder at what holds us all together.

Ambivalence

The main thing I've felt through my fiftieth year is the kind of having one foot in each world sense I vaguely remember from adolescence. I am eager to go forward and cash in on the rewards of growing up more completely, but I'm not quite ready to give up a more youthful attitude of dependency.

ELLEN

Many of us may feel as if we were forced to grow up way before our time. Perhaps we were the oldest daughter and were called upon to substitute for our mother in raising our siblings. Perhaps childhood traumas forced us to hide our vulnerabilities behind a mask that would make us appear better able to protect ourselves. Regardless of the reason, if we have a sense that we never had a proper childhood, we may find ourselves resistant to a second coming of age now, despite a yearning to be in the present with our true age.

We may need to give more recognition to the feelings of the child within us in order to release ourselves from the desire for dependency, for wanting someone else to take care of us. We are the adult who can take care of this child, and by so doing, we move into the mature adulthood we deserve and desire.

My ambivalence resolves when I have seen both sides of my conflict.

Age Stereotypes

Shortly after moving in, I went out and found her [my landlady and neighbor], barefoot, dressed in a halter top and shorts, energetically sloshing tar over leaky spots on the roof of her house. She was seventy-eight at the time. I realized that no stereotype of older women could account for Jackie.

PAMELA VALOIS

The more we observe and get to know vigorous, resplendent older women, the easier it is to defy the age stereotypes. But in a culture that is increasingly age segregated, where we have seniors living in separate housing, sometimes even separate communities that do not permit children, many of us know fewer and fewer people who are not of our own generation. We have to make a conscious effort to build and maintain relationships with elders, who provide us with living examples of our own future.

It is in the nature of a stereotype that we perceive those elders we know who are leading fruitful lives as rare exceptions, people who defy the norm. By doing this we discount them. We must count them and allow them to inspire us.

I look around today at all the vigorous elders I have known in my life.

Domination

To heal the world, and heal ourselves in the process, we must understand both how we internalize domination and how we can foster freedom. We must understand how we internalize each aspect of the self-hater and develop techniques for ridding ourselves of internalized domination. We must envision situations of liberation so that we can create them.

STARHAWK

We all have internalized, at least to some extent, the negative attitudes of our culture about aging. How can we recognize self-hate and not allow it to influence our choices and directions?

The first step is awareness. We must listen for this voice and register what it is saying. Does it say, "Look at your wrinkled baggy skin. You should do something about that?" Or, "You shouldn't associate with those older people. These younger ones are more like you." Or, "Knee surgery, so what. I'm going to get out there and ski no matter what. My age is not going to hold me back."

We speak back to this voice by taking the freedom to be our age and enjoy it. We moderate our activities when we know this will benefit us. We seek role models of older women who help us envision the rewards of the ripening years before us.

I recognize internalized negative messages so that I can part with them.

Perfection

The chief sign of pursuit of perfection is obsession. Obsession occurs when all the psychic energy, which ought to be distributed among the various parts of the personality in an attempt to harmonize them, is focused on one area of the personality to the exclusion of everything else.

MARION WOODMAN

Obsession freezes us. It leaves no room for spontaneity, for the discovery of our individual needs and desires and of the ways to meet and satisfy them. Why are we driven to obsess in the pursuit of perfection? Are we still trying to satisfy someone else?

We are not designed for perfection but to move toward wholeness and completeness. The very nature of addiction takes us away from any chance to achieve this wholeness by creating an obsessive concentration on one aspect of ourselves.

Midlife is a time when it appeals to us to seek balance. It is a time of appraisal in which we can choose to become mindful of obsessive thoughts and let them go rather than responding to them. We can also laugh at our desires for perfection. Having lived this long without achieving perfection, we cease to be duped.

I see the foolishness of the pursuit of perfection.

Pessimism

No pessimist ever discovered the secrets of the stars, or sailed to an uncharted land, or opened a new heaven to the human spirit.

HELEN KELLER

To believe something good lies ahead of us allows us to carry ourselves with lightness of being. To believe the opposite weights us with dread. When we walk in dread we barely look up. We discover very little. We are poised defensively for the arrival of bad news. The worst is bound to happen, and we had best be prepared for it. It seems the wider our heart is open, the greater we will be hurt. We do not want that, so we live curled up around our dire predictions.

Midlife is a time when we can stop and take a look at how our lives have gone. Even though we have encountered our share of troubles, we have survived. How much have we missed out on by cloaking ourselves in an attitude of pessimism? How much more are we willing to miss out on in the future by adhering to this attitude? When we take an honest look we see that despite our attitude, life seems to want to work out favorably where possible. And isn't it time we take this to encourage ourselves to become greater optimists?

Today, I leave my pessimistic attitude in the dump.

Fate

We are not really masters of our fate. We don't really direct our lives unaided and unobstructed. Our being is subject to all the chances of life.

KATHERINE ANNE PORTER

Surely we have seen people severely injured by an unfortunate fate. We may even number ourselves among these people and wonder what we might have been able to achieve had certain ill-fated incidents not come our way. Regardless of these feelings, however, we have to work with the gestalt of who we are today.

Whatever misfortunes have occurred, we can also recognize the resources we have acquired in dealing with them. Our pain has given depth to our vision. Our poverty has taught us to value nonmaterial gifts. Wherever obstacles have been laid down, we have found ways to scale them. No doubt we could have gone further or moved faster if we had been given better equipment to start with. Yet let us be satisfied that we are doing what we can do, within our fate.

I give my attention to the things I can change today and not to the things I cannot.

Acceptance

One cannot escape one's fate; the whole pain of it must be accepted, and one day the infinitely simple solution comes.

MARIE-LOUISE VON FRANZ

Some of us walk through the first half of life as if we are in a dream or a fantasy. We do battle with our demons, but we have little chance to express ourselves except in fantasy. Midlife offers us a good chance to come to a turning point, to accept the whole pain of our fate, and to reach our hands out toward something we love. Then we discover the spontaneity we were missing throughout the first half.

We who awaken in this way, who have had to travel a long way within ourselves to find life, know the meaning of life. We have the capacity to see the pain in others. We live with a full consciousness, awake to the moment. We reconcile the grief over what may feel like lost years by embracing the meaning of our suffering. Our fate has been given to us. So has the solution.

As soon as I accept my life, spontaneity flows from me.

Sexism

> Woman are not forgiven for aging. Robert Redford's lines of distinction are my old-age wrinkles.
>
> **JANE FONDA**

Imagine a world in which women with deeply wrinkled faces are considered distinguished—a world in which we say her face shows her to have lived and loved and suffered and developed compassion. Imagine in this same world that men with deeply wrinkled faces are considered frail and fragile. We try to keep them out of the spotlight for they reflect the vulnerability of our humanity, the side that we do not like featured on television.

Nowhere in the gender war do women come out as far ahead as we do in our longevity. But have we not earned equal distinction by putting in our time, as men have? Is there any reason why Robert Redford's wrinkles should earn him extra, while Jane Fonda's might devalue her? Let us recognize the sexism that permeates our notions about aging and strive to put it to rest.

I take the distinction my wrinkles have earned me.

Maturity

In youth we learn; in age
we understand.

MARIE EBNER-
ESCHENBACH

When we watch babies exploring, we
see very strikingly how learning is accomplished through constant experi-
mental trials. At the age when we know
nothing, we try everything. As we learn, we become more discriminating in our search. Otherwise life would be immeasur-
ably tiresome.

It is not as if we one day reach an age of understanding
and no longer have anything to learn. We are students of life
until the moment of death. But we do, in midlife, notice that
a transition has occurred. Where we once looked further
afield for answers, we now look within. Often we find the answer is there, provided our knowledge has been integrated.

*I appreciate my reservoir of knowledge and my
developing ability to call upon it for edification.*

Existence

Two things I have been without here: mirrors and clocks. At first it was so hard. It was an instinct to want to know how I looked; or perhaps I wanted to be able to catch glimpses of myself, just in passing, to reassure myself that I existed. That is what mirrors do; and also, I have decided, what clocks do.

JOAN BARFOOT

We depend a great deal on feedback to confirm who we are. Joan Barfoot's heroine goes out to live alone in a cabin in the woods to determine who she is without the constellation of her family around her. She faces the disorienting adjustment of living without clocks and mirrors. Let us try a day of living without clocks and mirrors.

Without clocks and mirrors we must look inward to confirm ourselves. We see immediately how much we have neglected to make a practice of this, how much definition we have taken from external sources. Especially in midlife it is important for us to take guidance from the images that reside deep within us. The primitive knowledge of the Wise Woman is there, a part of our heritage, as is the direction available from our heart.

Today, I free myself from outer reflection and seek my inward reflection.

Ageism

I begin to see that I myself am aging, was always aging, and that only powerful forces could have kept me from confronting so obvious a fact, or kept me—from self-interest alone—from working to change the social and economic realities of older women.

CYNTHIA RICH

We breathe the air of ageism throughout our lives. It motivates us to pass for younger whenever possible, to look away from the fate of our elders as if we are not going to be like them some day, and often to miss the riches of midlife. It does not serve women well to be infected with this ageism. It keeps us from working for changes to improve the conditions of older women, who we will inevitably become.

How, then, can we cease to perpetuate it? Our first step is awareness. We must recognize the attitudes that are diminishing to aging women. We must recognize these attitudes both as they are held and expressed by others and also as we carry them within ourselves. With this awareness we can begin to right the false conceptions of power, which give the upper hand to youth. We can avoid age-passing, which keeps us from the development of our true self.

Today, I wake up to the way ageism defines me and throw off its shackles.

Beauty

The moonlight animated the lines in her face. I wondered if thirty years before, when she was an eager girl dreaming of poetry, that face had been as beautiful as it was now. Whatever trials she had known she had transformed into tranquility.

ANZIA YEZIERSKA

When we gaze upon another out of love, we see the beauty of their whole being, not beauty as it has been defined and redefined to us through fashion or the style of the times. We see how a person has grown into herself, how she has taken grace into her stride, or aged with a certain sparkle in her eyes, or shows in her face the troubles that have deepened and anchored her knowledge of self.

Those moments when we look at and take in another fully are precious ones. They show us the truth of a being. They mirror the truth of *our* being. Beauty is not in classical lines or unmarred skin or elegant eyelashes; it is in life shining through, sometimes in the witnessing of someone's shed tear, sometimes in the smile of a stranger whom we pass on the street.

When my eyes are open I see beauty all around me.

Crone Persona

Hekate—like Hebe and Teleia—is Changing Woman. But the Crone persona most especially models *healing and transformation*. . . . One participates in Her essence—one gets Her power—when one responds to and enters into the ongoing transformation within all the moments, days, and seasons, as well as the entirety of one's life.

DONNA WILSHIRE

We can use the modeling of mythological figures to guide us to our wisdom. The Crone's gifts come from honoring the cycle of birth-death-rebirth. This cycle is occurring within us as well as all around us.

The winter is a period of darkness. Plants go to stillness. Animals hibernate. Menopause is a similar period of transition. The fertile woman within us is dying. We mourn her. We let her die. The Wise Woman is born from her death. We do not always recognize her within us at first. But gradually we do as she takes root and grows.

I flow with the transformations of the seasons of my body.

Attitude Toward Our Body

Our physicality—which always and everywhere includes our spirituality, mentality, emotionality, social institutions and processes—is a microform of all physicality. Each of us reflect, in our attitudes toward our bodies and the bodies of other planetary creatures and plants, our inner attitude toward the planet. And, as we believe, so we act.

PAULA GUNN ALLEN

What is our attitude toward our body? Is it loving, tender, and respectful? Or is it rejecting, denying, and critical? Do we dislike our body for being in a state of change? Do we act as if it is betraying us by aging? Let us note the correlation between how we treat our body and how we treat other planetary creatures and plants. When we spend time tending other life carefully, we discover a more compassionate attitude toward ourself.

If we look at our attitude toward our body and see what we would like to change, then we will be able to do something about it. For instance, we can make a daily practice of treating ourself more gently. We can honor our body as the sacred vessel it is—always there for us, always present to carry us—by feeding ourself well and granting ourself enough rest. We can focus our attention on healing whatever part of us is ailing.

I honor my body as but one planetary creature and treat it with the great respect that it deserves.

Courage

Much as we associate courage with the dramatic heroic event, isn't it true that the times we draw upon it with the greatest need are often the times of our quiet distress, when we simply don't know how we are going to get through? And don't we always find it then, a hidden reserve? Sometimes we find it through sharing our pain with another, or through prayer or meditation, in which we visualize a relationship with some greater power in the universe.

Sometimes we need the courage of getting through one moment to the next not so much at a time of distress as simply one of not knowing. For example, we are creating something—a painting, a piece of writing—and we cease to have vision. Our courage comes when we wait and trust that we will see again. Or perhaps we are performing an assembly-line job. We are tired and hit a great wall, feeling, *I cannot do this one more time*. But we must. And somehow we muster the courage to get through to the next minute—a great victory.

Courage is not something that only comes to other people. I recognize the moments when my own courage carries me through.

Reverie

To make a prairie it takes
a clover and one bee,
One clover, and a bee,
And revery.
The revery alone will do,
If bees are few.

EMILY DICKINSON

What is reverie? Why do we need it, and what do we miss when we go without it? To create something we need to be able to imagine it. We need to give it the energy of reverence and devotion. Nothing comes into our life without prior visualization of some sort. Sometimes we dream a thing, sometimes we find ourselves drawn toward a desire—to travel to a certain land, to visit an old relative who might not have long to live, to take ourselves to the top of a mountain.

Giving honor to our dreams and desires takes us closer to the fulfillment of them. Letting ourselves have the time for reverie, not letting ourselves be stopped by some authoritarian voice that says, "What a waste of time, you are not doing anything," feeds our soul and lets our vision focus with greater clarity.

Today, I entertain the gifts of the imagination that reverie affords me.

Luminosity

Life is a luminous halo,
a semi-transparent
envelope surrounding us
from the beginning.

VIRGINIA WOOLF

Life seems to be always watching over us, even as it eludes us, even as we struggle and strain to see what it is all about. Sometimes we see no light, yet others looking at us might see us surrounded by light. When we weep, we feel as if our eyes are shrouded with darkness. But after our weeping, someone may tell us that our eyes are sparkling with light. To reconcile these differences, we must realize that life is sometimes beyond our inner perception of it.

Now life is ushering us through midlife. Certain natural events such as the physical changes of menopause, quite possibly the death of a parent, the exodus of our children, alter our perception of ourselves. Many of us have a time of feeling as if we are lost on our journey. We question where we have been and where we are going. But the north star is there, still present in the northern sky. Light still illuminates us, even when we cannot see it.

I notice the luminosity in others and trust they are my mirrors.

Constitution

I know I have the body of a weak and feeble woman, but I have the heart and stomach of a king, and of a king of England too.

QUEEN ELIZABETH I

Haven't we all known women who are frail, and yet, throughout great travail, they endure with the most steely constitutions? Many women cleverly learn to conserve their energy to get through a day of caring for several young children, perhaps going to work as well, saving a few moments toward the end of the day to feed themselves a small portion of individual connection, an energy with which to awaken for the next day.

As we grow older and become more vulnerable to the frailties of our bodies, we notice, ironically, that we simultaneously experience ourselves as stronger than we've ever been before. The strength is not in our muscles but in our inner being and conviction. Our hearts and our stomachs have endured upsets and proved themselves capable of great range and resilience. We have learned to hear them and to attend them as they carry us along.

My strong heart and my strong stomach lend me
a feeling of unity and power today.

Troubles

> I would perhaps have more actual troubles, but I'd have fewer imaginary ones.
>
> **NADINE STAIR**

As we move through our years we become better at distinguishing our imaginary troubles from our actual ones. We have had time to work through much of our past, which keeps interjecting itself into the present until it captures our attention. As we have done this work, we have found it freeing.

When we are down to our actual troubles, we may still have a lot to handle. Yet we discover that handling them is simply life—we are not being singled out for more than our share. It does not do us any good to make comparisons to our neighbors. Nor does it enrich our lives to focus on when we will be finished with these troubles. The moment we are in now is the vital one. The attitude with which we face our troubles can lift us if we let it include humor, hope, and room for the unexpected.

Today, I turn my energy to my actual troubles, leaving my imaginary ones to fall away.

Peace

African violets in the
    light
breathing, in a
    breathing universe. I
    want strong peace,
    and delight,
    the wild good.

MURIEL RUKEYSER

Do we know what we want? Do we
allow ourselves to go for it? An advantage of growing older is that we have
accumulated more experience. We have
tried different directions to find what
satisfies us. Perhaps we have pursued
more than one career. Perhaps we have
sought out a series of mates, discovering different aspects of
ourselves along the way.

Increasingly we find our way to the same conclusion—
that we want peace and delight. In our earlier years we may
have sought to fill ourselves with other people. We may have
tried to find someone else to complete us. By now we have
the wisdom to realize we are complete unto ourselves. We
find peace within. We seek joy both in us and through the
company of those in whom we delight.

Because I value peace, to me peace comes.

Rootedness

A tree puts down its roots before it sends its shoots up and out.

JUDITH JAMISON

Midlife is an expansive time because we have our roots down. Even if we move to a new geographic area, we bring our psychic roots along—we know who we are, what we value, and what principles we choose to follow.

From these roots we shoot up and out. We consolidate our energy, which we once might have squandered. During our menopause there are times when we feel our life constrict, as if in hibernation, burrowing inward and keeping still. This is a perfectly natural state, part of the contraction-expansion rhythm of life. We contract to gestate and prepare for our next expansion.

In our midlife expansion we grow more at home with ourselves. Aspects of ourselves we once thought we needed to change we merely need to love instead. We no longer need to listen to the critical inner voice that sometimes holds us back.

I stand sturdy on my feet and feel my rootedness.

Pain

What an incredible life I've had and how lucky I am and how easy it was—looking back. Of course while doing it, it wasn't easy; but maybe my whole life was easy in one way because all the pain was building toward something, and it did build toward something.

ROSEANNE BARR

Hindsight has a way of putting pain in its place. We can see as we look back that it moved us along, albeit haltingly. Without our wounds, how many of us would have gone deeper in our search for ourselves? Had we stayed on the surface, how much would we have missed?

At midlife we often see our energies converging. We see that we have successfully built toward something. Perhaps we are able to see who we are and what we want with clarity. We may have grown more comfortable living in our own skin. It may be that the world offers us opportunities to utilize our talents, and we are able to take them.

My pain has prodded me along on my journey.

Time

It is our inward journey that leads us through time—forward or back, seldom in a straight line, most often spiraling. Each of us is moving, changing, with respect to others. As we discover, we remember; remembering, we discover; and most intensely do we experience this when our separate journeys converge.

EUDORA WELTY

We live with our clocks set to the proper time, giving us orientation to the passage of our days. But simultaneously we experience time less linearly on our inward journey. We work for a long time toward resolution of some problem, then suddenly, like an unclogged ice jam, the problem breaks apart and we have a new flow.

We meet certain people who seem to be sent to greet us at a particular hour of our life. Perhaps we met them once before but walked right past them. When we are ready to learn, they appear to teach us. Or sometimes we sense someone has appeared to receive a lesson from us.

Each of us continues to uncover and discover and remember. In this way the thread of our life pulls through to make a tapestry. The older we grow, the more we can see of the tapestry, and yet we realize we know nothing of the mystery of time.

I see myself surfacing on a spiral of time.

Love

Why is the measure of
love loss?

**JEANETTE
WINTERSON**

We feel the value of love heightened in its absence or in its earliest appearance. When we fall in love with a new lover, or when we are provoked by our connection with a new friend, we are lit up by a sense of chemistry. Jung said that when two beings come together and there is a reaction, like two chemicals, each will be transformed by the experience.

After the early glow of love, it is harder for us to appreciate the deep value of our connection with another. We are often only provoked to know it fully when the one we love is removed from us. Then the depth of our loss informs us of how greatly we have cared for them and been buoyed by their caring for us. We discover how much we are all connected despite the fact that we are also very much alone.

By midlife we have enough experience with love not to wait for an ending before appreciating what we have. We can heighten our love daily because of our awareness.

*Love is a measure of the openness of my heart. I give
and receive it without taking it for granted.*

Beginnings

Nothing, of course,
begins at the time you
think it did.

LILLIAN HELLMAN

Does midlife begin at forty? Does old age begin at seventy? We gravitate toward these demarcations, but in fact life is more fluid than that. We who are in midlife now have an occasional glimpse of our old age. We pass through a moment in which we are old, a moment that seems very real. The expanse of all ages exists in the collective imagination, and we need only be willing to tap into that imagination.

Looking at our impulses to develop parts of ourselves that have seemingly lain dormant until now and to channel our vitality in new directions, we discover our desires were actually present long before. We always wanted to try our hand at watercolors. We've long yearned, in some unspoken way, to travel back to the land of our ancestors. We've always known we could be a good teacher of the work we love. The continuity of our impulses reveals itself as we venture forth to exercise them.

I see that the beginning for what I am starting to do now existed long before the doing.

Respect of Body

Bless your body always.
Speak no word of
condemnation about it.

REBECCA BEARD

Who is our most stalwart companion from birth right up to the moment of our death? Our body. She is with us always—in the moments we accept her, in the moments we reject her. She contains us. She embraces us. She carries us through every pain and expresses to us every pleasure. She deserves our greatest respect and ample caretaking.

At menopause we may wish our body belonged to someone else. We may perceive her as causing us trouble, but she is only containing our changes. Let us support her with our knowledge, with our caring, and with proper nourishment. Let us stay present inside her and allow her to be our guide.

*I have been blessed with my body; I receive this
blessing with gratitude and awe.*

True to Life

You see—to me—life and work are two things indivisible. It's only by being true to life that I can be true to art. And to be true to life is to be *good, sincere, simple, honest.*

KATHERINE MANSFIELD

What do we mean when we say, "Be true to life"? Do we mean follow closely the ways of our nature? Do we mean don't resist the flow of life but move in the direction it wants of us? Do we mean follow the principles we have discovered offer us a good life?

Sometimes we fail to be true to life because we are busy struggling to control things around us— the behavior of others, the inefficiencies of bureaucracy, or even bad weather. Meanwhile *our* life is going on without our full attention.

As we enter menopause bombarded with the message that we are done for, of course we will pause and wish to forestall this passage. But being true to life means opening up the gates of our resistance so that we can make this passage consciously, letting ourselves appreciate the alterations that occur in all our aspects—physical, emotional, intellectual, and spiritual.

To be true to life is to relax into who I am today.

Earth

When I realize how invigorating contact with the earth may sometimes be, I find myself wondering how humanity ever consented to come so far away from the jungle.

ELLEN GLASGOW

Contact with the earth is important. Even if we live in cities, we need to keep this connection. Our contact can come from a walk in a park or even from tending our houseplants. That touch of earth reminds us of our planetary relationship and how we as human beings are but one of the species supported by the Great Mother.

In autumn in northern climates, we now watch the plants and the grasses shrink back and die. We turn over our gardens, letting the dried-out plants decompose and feed back their nutrients. We prepare for our own dormant season as well, becoming quieter, perhaps looking deeper into our own dark recesses.

Menopause sometimes resembles November. It directs us to contain ourselves, to stay inward until we hatch with a new understanding of ourselves. Longer light will come our way when it is time.

I touch the earth each day in some small way.

Mastery

The great thing and the hard thing is to stick to things when you have outlived the first interest, and not yet got the second which comes with a sort of mastery.

JANET ERSKINE STUART

Often midlife is a time for taking on new interests or for attempting to actualize old interests that we have never given ourselves the time to explore. It can be difficult for many of us to become students again, newcomers, people in the position of not knowing. But we only learn by admitting we don't know how to do something. Our age does not keep us from taking up something entirely new, starting like a baby or a teenager would.

Let us say we have always had a desire to express ourselves through an art form, such as painting or playing the piano. Nothing but our own internal censor can stop us from beginning our lessons now and becoming a novice again at midlife.

After we have overcome that voice and begun, we encounter that difficult period when the thrill of initiation is over and mastery has not yet been accomplished. We wonder why we ever thought we could do this. This is the moment for our commitment to shine through.

I venture from first lessons down the path to mastery.

Sleep

When action grows
unprofitable, gather
information; when
information grows
unprofitable, sleep.

URSULA K. LE GUIN

Many of us discover that we require
more sleep as we come into menopause.
At first we may resist this, fearing that
giving in to this message of our body
will be a sign of defeat. But sooner or
later we realize that we owe it to our body to grant it what it
needs. Our increased sleep may prove quite profitable, both
by resting us and by preparing us for the next stage of the
journey.

Sleep is a time of gestation—both literal sleep and down-
time when we ponder and daydream over what vaguely troubles us, resting from the need for decision or deliverance. It is
a mode in which we become receptive. We stop being in
charge. The messages of our unconscious can then reach
through to us. The feelings we may have pushed aside can
find their proper place. As we reconstitute ourselves, we
gather energy for action. And when we are ready, this cycle
begins anew.

I recognize the great profits of the time I lie dormant.

Perspective

A sense of standing at a peak looking at a wide expanse of land. Perspective. Distance. Pattern becomes important. There is more of a sense of how it all fits together. A softness to this view.

CARMEN DE MONTEFLORES

By midlife we have traveled around certain blocks many times. Now, with bifocals, our vision of some things becomes more acute. Perhaps we can see a purpose that eluded us earlier. Perhaps we can see how, even when we experience frustration, we are learning what we needed to know. Perhaps our compassion helps us see that paths we followed that seemed like "mistakes" were not mistakes at all, but necessary parts of the journey.

Knowing life's pattern, we are more apt to say "This too shall pass" when we encounter difficult feelings or trying times. We recognize that we are in charge of less than we once thought, and this becomes a relief rather than a dread. We are content with our inability to know what's around each corner, since the outcome will be revealed to us in time.

I appreciate having the perspective to see the tapestry of patterns that play in my life.

Historical Perspective

Youth is something very
new: twenty years ago
no one mentioned it.

COCO CHANEL

Although we now have to add a few
years to this comment, it is useful to remember that fifty or sixty years ago no
one mentioned youth. The growth of
the youth industry has paralleled the development of visual
communications media. In the 1940s and 1950s, ads for
household products were directed at the mature woman of
the house. Then they became directed at the young, glamorous woman. Now we are encouraged to buy a product so we
will be able to see ourselves as young and glamorous by association.

While society's focus on youth has brought progress by
giving greater recognition to the rights of children, ultimately, we need to have greater respect for all ages. Then the
glorification of youth as a stage we should all stay in will be
able to fade away.

*I deflate youth to its proper place in the long
continuum of a lifetime.*

Tyranny

Under conditions of
tyranny it is far easier to
act than to think.

HANNAH ARENDT

Is there a tyranny of age in our age?
Indeed, are we acting when it would be
wise to stop and think? What voices
inside us tell us we should act, look, and
be younger than we are? Who does this benefit? Surely not
us, for it only serves to keep us apart from the loving acceptance we need to support ourselves properly.

The main instrument of tyranny is control, exerted
through fear and diminishment, making the one controlled
feel humiliated, terrorized, trivialized. We learn to be obedi-
ent, and we use these tactics on ourselves when listening to
the voices that tell us what we *should* do.

We will feel much more positive about our aging if we
stop to notice these voices and begin to talk back to them. By
talking back, we develop a dialogue that stands to help our
sisters as well as ourselves. We say: Each and every age is a
fine one. We say: Let us appreciate and enjoy the riches of the
year that is mine today. We celebrate each birthday and the
life that has been given to us.

I talk back to the youth tyrant residing in me.

Moods

> What are moods? Are they the grace and perfume of existence, or are they the uncertain shoals on which we run aground and perish? Are they to be cultivated as the finest flowers of existence, or are they to be rooted out as the weeds "that choke the true Word"?
>
> **RUTH BENEDICT**

As we go through extreme bouts of moodiness in menopause, many of us become more aware of the influence of moods. One day we are grouchy for no reason. Another day we are ebullient. Why? We're not sure. On the ebullient day moods do seem to be the "grace and perfume of existence"; on the blue day, they seem a scheme to sink us.

When we are under the clouds, we tend to exaggerate the negative. Life is not good, never has been, never will be. However, our wisdom tells us that moods pass through like weather. At the end of a series of cloudy days, our spirits will be lifted again by the warmth and sparkle of the sun's rays.

With all due respect for my feelings, I listen to my wisdom when caught under a series of dark clouds.

Loneliness

Loneliness is the poverty
of self; solitude is the
richness of self.

MAY SARTON

What a great range of wealth—from poverty to riches—exists in the state of aloneness. This great range also exists when we are together with others. For where we stand on the spectrum always derives from our inner position. We can be lonely when we are alone and just as lonely in the middle of a crowd.

Many of us feel lonely in menopause because we feel set off from others who are not in a similar state. No one can understand us, we complain. Our husbands aren't experiencing the same physical changes that we are having during midlife. Perhaps it is important to listen to this message without resentment, to grant ourselves some time in solitude to honor ourselves and the differences we are experiencing.

When we are afraid of being set apart by our differences, it is usually because we are not at peace with ourselves. Let us sit still quietly long enough to pass through our apprehension, listening for the sense of self that will eventually emerge to fill us.

*I recognize my loneliness as a distance from myself
and come closer.*

Suffering

Seeing pain as a part of the process enlarges the perspective that sees it only as a sign of pathology and a stigma. It permits empathy with the suffering and permits natural healing. It permits suffering through to gestate a new solution in its own way and its own time.

— SYLVIA BRINTON PERERA

By midlife most of us have learned this to be true—that seeing suffering through will gestate a new solution. This is not the either/or solution, the one that comes out of black-and-white thinking, the one that says if I choose A, I must sacrifice B entirely. This is the solution that is born of opposites, showing us the middle ground we were not capable of seeing while clinging to our polarized position.

Pain, whatever the degree, is simply one of the givens in life. We are not unique when we have it, nor is there any chance of our avoiding it. Perhaps without it, we would not know peace or pleasure. Perhaps without it we would seek no solace from another. Let us accept it as a valuable part of our process and yield to suffering when we need to, seeing that this is all a natural part of life.

I feel the pain and let my suffering show me the way.

Life in the Moment

A surprising (and surprisingly unacknowledged) amount of life is spent in a sort of abstracted suspension, as if in anticipation of some miraculous, scarcely imagined event which, if and when it ever comes, then leaves us bereft, painfully nostalgic. I've said it elsewhere too: how hard it is to live in time!

RACHEL HADAS

How often we live in anticipation of some grandness or in nostalgia over the good times of our lives that have already passed. Meanwhile we miss the grandness of the day we are being given. We fail to hear the birds sing. We fail to feel the caress of the sun on our faces or to let music enter our soul. Even the hug or the touch of another can be received rotely, as if we did not receive anything at all.

Periodically, we realize the great loss we are accruing when we are too busy or distracted to be present. We realign ourselves and become aware of our intent to live in the now. Most often we are richly rewarded in a very immediate way, for our life becomes instantaneously more worthwhile and full of daily stimulation. It is a mystery why we still tend to slip back into the old mode of anticipation, but unless we bring a daily consciousness to this resolve, we lose it all too easily.

Each day I remind myself anew to live this day while it is here.

Attitude

If you can't change your
fate, change your
attitude.

AMY TAN

We are fated to grow older. We are not fated to do it grumpily, resentfully, fearfully, or even glowingly. We cannot always control or choose whether we will encounter illness or disability with our aging or remain in good health. What we can choose is the attitude with which we encounter our fate.

With an attitude of acceptance we have more energy for interacting with whatever obstacles present themselves. We accept them and work with them rather than against them. Many of us first rail and resist the changes in our bodies and our psyches, acting as if they have betrayed us and so we will reject them. When the storm of our anger has passed, we can see the underlying fear of our vulnerability.

We can change our attitude in a second. Watch what happens when we do.

*I exert the choice that is in my control—the decision
to take an attitude that can help me.*

Fear

"Have you noticed?" whispers Grandmother Growth. "Your hot flashes and menstrual irregularities disrupt your normal patterns, make openings for your buried fears to emerge. Approach with curiosity; let your fears bring you gifts of self-awareness."

GRANDMOTHER GROWTH (SUSUN S. WEED)

Always we have fear in the midst of change. Terrain that was once solid footing now becomes shaky beneath our feet. We wish for it to become steady again quickly, as if we are walking out on a footbridge, tempted to go back to where we embarked from and hold fast to the old ground a little longer rather than to be suspended with uncertainty. But in menopause our body tells us we might as well make the best of things, for we must continue across the footbridge once we have begun.

Having our buried fears emerge presents us the opportunity to face and comprehend them, to release old ghosts, and to clean out our psychic cobwebs. Many of our unconscious demons have been held hostage while we moved through life as oblivious as we could. As we meet them one by one, we will be enlarged in our wisdom.

I let fear guide me to the dark places where illumination can make me whole.

Getting a Start

I got myself a start by
giving myself a start.

MADAM C. J.
WALKER

By midlife we can look back on a fair amount of accumulated experience. Surely we have gotten a start in certain areas of our lives. The energy of transition may bring us low and make us feel passive, necessarily, for we must slow down to take new direction. In the midst of this it may be difficult for us to remember how many of our starts have been facilitated by us—by our willingness and by our actions. It will help us if we make an honest appraisal of our past.

If we look carefully, we will notice that periods of dormancy lead up to periods of direction and growth. We might think of a seed germinating, storing the energy to shoot up its new growth into a blooming plant. When we are in the dormant/receptive phase, we are prone to feeling as if we are more dependent on others than we really are. We begin to believe that we are waiting for someone else to give us a start. We are really waiting for ourselves to catch up and be ready.

I give myself a start when I am ready to begin anew.

Women as Heroes

I am convinced that women need a new hero myth, a new way of thinking about who we really are, what we can become, and the tasks we confront in a world overwhelmed with escalating social, political, and environmental crises. . . . [One] that teaches us to claim, not suppress, the power of our femininity.

KATHLEEN NOBLE,
PH.D.

We were raised on heroic myths and stories in which only the male character took the heroic journey. Female heroes tended to be the reliable homemaker/caretakers of the male heroes. Now we have come through a feminist revolution in which we have written and told our own stories, seeing and heralding the heroism inherent in showing up for daily life. But do we need more?

Perhaps we need to envision the woman hero who can lead the world to greater peace, using her feminine powers to take leadership in the world. Perhaps that woman hero would offer more options for resolving conflicts than going to war. Perhaps in that hero we can see the wisdom of the Crone, which is developing in each and every one of us.

*I weave visions of new women heroes,
myself among them.*

Sleeplessness

With no understanding, no way of knowing that the death we shiver against in the wee hours could be symbolic or even the first stage of a new beginning, sleep eludes us and waking dread takes its place. No one tells us that it might be our old way of being in the world that must die to make way for the new.

JANE R. PRÉTAT

If we honestly examine our life experience, we know that this is true, that always in times of major transition we have woken in dread, fearing death, dreaming death, knowing death, and fearing the cycle would not continue. We were being born anew even as we wrestled with an unnerving sense of aloneness and loss.

We are far from our adolescence now, yet we may still remember nights so bound up with our changes that we felt we had not slept a wink. With our youthful resiliency, we were better able to shrug off our fatigue the next morning. Midlife sleeplessness seems more tragic because we need our sleep more. Still, it helps to relieve our anxiety if we recognize that an important passage is being made whenever we suffer those difficult nights. Let us not treat them only as nuisances but as important steps in our descent to the dark in which we are rebirthing ourselves.

In the dreaded darkness, I leave behind the old.

Inner Space

... I find excitement in [the journey's] solitary, edge-of-the-world sensation of entering new territory with the wind whistling past my ears. Who would have imagined, for instance, that I, once among the most externalized of people, would now think of meditation as a tool of revolution (without self-authority, how can we keep standing up to external authority?) or consider inner space more important to explore than outer space?

GLORIA STEINEM

Not uncommonly, women who have been geared up and expressing themselves for years as activists discover the need to go inward to seek their own "self-authority" at some time during their midlife transition. Many of us are initially frightened of this journey. If our inner space is relatively unexplored territory, we feel lost when we enter it. We do not recognize its contours. We do not know how to behave in it. Give us the street and a bullhorn and we can ask people to follow us. But give us our own inner darkness and mystery and we have no idea how to begin a dialogue.

Meditation provides a structure for staying still long enough to recognize our interior. There are other forms we can use as well. For instance, we can review and ponder our dreams, or dialogue with our dream or fantasy figures in our journals, letting them speak to us as inner guides.

Today, I turn to inner space for self-authority.

Tears

The fact that I cry every day is liberating, but the hot flashes are from hell.

SALLY

Many of us cried as children and then shut off our tears for many years as adults. Perhaps nothing short of a major funeral was capable of moving us to tears, or perhaps we cried only during sentimental movies. We were adults in charge of children, tending to their tears. We were grown-ups who had learned to keep a close hold on our feelings. We, who have been like this, may be surprised to find menopause flooding us with daily tears as if to make up for all that time.

Crying is a great healer. Our tears give expression to our sorrow, and a plenitude of sorrow is something we all have. Perhaps menopause is a time for equilibrium, to bring us up to the present emotionally. So that for every tear stored up, we are now provided an exit. We are not crying out of self-pity but because our old walls have crumbled and our new, second adulthood seeks a way to integrate our self with all our feelings.

The free flow of my tears is cleansing me.

Accumulation

> The great thing about getting older is that you don't lose all the other ages you've been.
>
> **MADELEINE L'ENGLE**

Our wrinkles add up. So does the substantial nature of all the experience we have accumulated. It fills us where we once thought we would always feel empty. We let go of our youth but our memory bank is filled with it. And this builds a bridge between us and the youth of today, regardless of whether their appearance alienates us or not. We know their innocence. We know their desire for a distinguishing rebellion.

When we achieve something now, we know enough to take it in. When we achieved the same thing in our younger years, we might have dismissed it, saying, "If I managed to do this, it must have been easy," even though it wasn't easy. When we were given recognition, we might have thought only, "More, give me more, I haven't gotten enough yet."

At last we have reached an age in which we allow things to add up. We receive a new fullness and contentment from this. There is no hole in our bucket. Our accumulated experience fills it to the brim.

All my years fill me today.

Arrival of Aging

Age seldom arrives smoothly or quickly. It's more often a succession of jerks.

JEAN RHYS

One morning we wake up with a crick in our hip that leads to a jerky gait. We have to move around the house a bit before we can stand up straight. We encounter a health problem associated with middle age, such as gum disease. When our dentist breaks the news, we are surprised to have reached a juncture associated with age.

Menopause arrives in fits for many of us. Some of us encounter flooding periods just when we think they are going to stop coming entirely. Some of us are just as shocked when we miss our first one. We react to our bodies as if they are forsaking us.

Our aging arrives in a succession of jerks, prodding our awareness. Our acceptance is more likely to sail in quietly on the smooth sea that comes after the turbulence of resistance.

Only a jerky arrival is capable of awakening me to my aging.

Unacceptable Conditions

I've arrived at this outermost edge of my life by my own actions. Where I am is thoroughly unacceptable. Therefore, I must stop doing what I've been doing.

ALICE KOLLER

We often do not change until we arrive at some unacceptable, outermost edge. For instance, we may wrack up debts until we are going crazy from handling the financial crisis we are in. We may reject all the people around us as either too good for us or not good enough before we come to reckon with our own fear of people. Whenever we reach that outermost edge and realize we do not like where we have found ourselves, we can begin to take action toward change.

Our midlife is a time for change, for stopping to look at where we are. Do we find ourselves in a place that is acceptable or unacceptable? For instance, are we doing the work we want to be doing? Having the relationships we want to be having? We may have been afraid to look at the place that is unacceptable because looking provoked our shame. Let us not shame ourselves into inaction but assess more coolly and begin to conceive the small actions that will move us to a new place.

I accept the unacceptable by taking steps toward change.

Energy

Life engenders life.
Energy creates energy. It
is by spending oneself
that one becomes rich.

SARAH BERNHARDT

Saving judiciously in order to provide for one's older years is not the same as hoarding. Hoarding always stops life's energy from flowing because it is a wish for accumulation: *Let us keep everything that comes to us so that we will fill up*. We never get enough when we are thinking this way, for only by spending and giving do we remain a part of the cycling of life's energy.

All life manifests through energy. Our physical vitality is part of our energy. Our money is part of our energy. Our intellectual liveliness is part of our energy. When we give of our energy freely, we receive the gift of energy coming back to us. It may not be in the same form. Sometimes we may even fail to recognize it, but we must trust in its return and lift within ourselves any gates that block us from receiving it.

If our energy feels low during our menopause, let us trust that we are being given the stillness to transform.

My energy is bountiful when I give of it freely.

Tranquility

Like water which can clearly mirror the sky and the trees only so long as its surface is undisturbed, the mind can only reflect the true image of the Self when it is tranquil and wholly relaxed.

INDRA DEVI

As we seek to right ourselves in mid-life—to align our priorities to meet our needs, to respect the changes in our energy, and to open new parts of ourselves that have been closed—we cherish the tranquility that allows us to see the reflection of the "true image of the Self."

For it is from seeing this reflection that we can choose our directions with confidence and follow a path as if we held a compass before us.

How do we find this tranquility? We must learn to be still and quiet. Some of us practice a form of meditation to reach our quiet center. Some of us pull weeds in a garden until all our distractions are plucked away. Some of us watch the repetitive motion of the waves of the ocean. Once we reach our still-point, images form before our eyes like visions. They may show us where we are going. They may simply hold us in peace, as we are.

Tranquility is a precious gift I treasure when it comes to me.

Success

People fail forward to success.

MARY KAY ASH

Do we all have some ideal picture in our minds of the successful person? Perhaps they are ascending a long staircase, sometimes two steps at a time, certainly not faltering, turning back only to take bows at certain landings. Yet this ideal does not match our experience, even in the areas of our lives where we feel the most successful.

Success often appears around a corner when we least expect it, after we have put in plenty of work and let go of dogged control and the wish to make a particular thing happen. Often we feel as if we have hit the dry bottom of our well of resources, only to find ourselves renewed and able to spring forward and enjoy some new success.

I let go of expectations of success and become receptive to noticing when it comes to me.

Creativity

Living in a state of psychic unrest, in a Borderland, is what makes poets write and artists create.

GLORIA ANZALDUA

Menopause can be a highly creative time for us. We are charged with psychic unrest by being in this "Borderland," both the borderland of coming to age and reckoning with what this means within us and the borderland of facing a prevalent ageism in our society that would render us invisible and without our wisdom and power.

Creativity is required to make a proper home for ourselves in these circumstances. We must make ourselves seen and heard when others have learned not to see or hear our full value. When we go down deep in search of the ways to express all our multifaceted dimensions, we find our creativity, and through its use, edify not only ourselves but others.

From my borderland I bloom like a wildflower that grows from a split in a rock.

The Ideal

The Real is the sole
foundation of the Ideal.

GRACE AGUILAR

On what do we base the ideal? The real.
Otherwise we are talking about un-
grounded, pie-in-the-sky fantasies.

The ideal offers us a destination, a point to which to move
and grow. As we enter midlife, we need to imagine our ideal fulfillment of this passage, the ways we'd like to capture and de-
marcate the essence of this experience. Our ideal can be based
on what we learn of the accumulated experience of our older
sisters. What do they have to say about life at fifty, at sixty, at
seventy? And our ideal is based upon what we desire to grow
into—the essential positive aspects of age, such as wisdom.

We distinguish an ideal from the impulse to perfection-
ism. An ideal is simply the picture we posit as desirable. We
must be quick to recognize our humanity when we fall short
of reaching it and refrain from using this as a reason for berat-
ing ourselves. There will always be rocky places on our path.
We continue to climb in spite of them, keeping in mind our
ideal, and learning patience.

*I allow myself an ideal picture of moving into older
ages rather than simply cringing at the sense
of lost youth.*

Crones

I have known four or five Crones, two of them men. I have gone to them when I thought I couldn't go any further. Their love was palpable. No advice. Simply being, saying almost nothing. I know I was totally seen and totally understood. They could constellate my own inner healer because they could see me as I am.

MARION WOODMAN

Two missions that come to us in our middle life are to look toward learning to receive from Crones and to look toward becoming Crones.

What a gift it is to be seen in our full depth by another. Many of us have a good deal of trouble even seeing ourselves clearly. Especially as we change in midlife, we may encounter a period of feeling lost, as if we cannot locate ourselves, even though we are still living under the same sky with the same constellations above. This is a time when someone's silent *seeing* of us can help us to see and recognize ourselves.

The Crone's gift is wisdom, distilled from the collection of experience. Let us not be reluctant to tap it and to let it aide us in taking ourselves further.

I see in the Crones the acceptance that can be mine as I reconstitute myself.

Depression

One is free from depression when self-esteem is based on the authenticity of one's own feelings and not on the possession of certain qualities.

ALICE MILLER

Many women encounter depression as they go through menopause. At least some of this depression may be the way a person experiences losses, such as the diminution of youthful beauty and health or the death of loved ones. Yet there are others who experience these types of losses and mourn them without depression.

Depression pushes us down and attempts to hold us still for a while. It might seem as if a thick fog has taken over our lives and blocks us from seeing the far horizon. In severe forms it calls for treatment, but for many of us it provides a drag to our daily pace that orients us to look within. Especially at midlife, depression may want to exact something from us—attention to ourselves. Is our self-esteem based on the possession of certain qualities, like being hard working, good looking, or physically fit, in tip-top shape? Or does it come from a deeper sense of well-being within us? Our depression may want to guide us to pay more attention to the feelings within.

Today, if I am depressed, I will ask my depression what it might want of me.

Time in Aging

... time for me can be as long or as short as it always was, but we do not necessarily move forward in it in the same old way, and memories appear with such startling clarity that they can displace what we see in front of our eyes.

MARY MEIGS

There is a supposition that time passes more slowly in youth and speeds up with age. Yet if we look at time on a daily, moment-to-moment basis, we see the large variance in our perception of its passage. One morning passes as if it only contained an hour; another drags as if it were a whole day.

We see our elders spend more time remembering. We do not know exactly where they are or what they experience. Perhaps we think this tendency is making them dullards, while as Mary Meigs describes, they are living a vivid moment through memory. They are literally swept away by this.

No matter how fast or slow time goes for us, it becomes more precious as we realize that our years are limited. Apparently it will pass whether we do what we want to with our lives or not. Let us awaken as fully as we can to its passage.

Time does not necessarily speed up with aging,
but I become more aware of its passage.

Illness

Everyone who is born holds dual citizenship, in the kingdom of the well and in the kingdom of the sick. Although we all prefer to use only the good passport, sooner or later each of us is obliged, at least for a spell, to identify ourselves as citizens of that other place.

SUSAN SONTAG

All of us at some time encounter illness. What do we gain from our citizenship in that place? We learn to become centered in our body. Sometimes we are slowed down enough by our illness to ponder major decisions that we have busily avoided making. Sometimes our illness takes us inside to gestate new beginnings or to chew over some old, now useless or painful habits that we are ready to get rid of.

During our midlife years, many of us encounter a major illness for the first time. Breast cancer is becoming an epidemic in middle-aged or older women. Large numbers of women are suffering from chronic fatigue syndrome. Some of us encounter the onset of arthritis during our midlife years. Let us use our passport to this place, though it is not of our choosing, to good advantage. Traveling to any foreign country is an eye-opening experience. Let us open our eyes to see what our illness may have to show us.

I travel mindfully with my illnesses, letting them instruct me as the traveler.

Face

> Nature gives you the face you have when you are twenty. Life shapes the face you have at thirty. But it is up to you to earn the face you have at fifty.
>
> **COCO CHANEL**

At fifty our face has had time to form. If we have spent much of our time in bitterness, that look will come to show in our face. If we have walked through life in dismay and bewilderment, we will have a certain look that says we are still seeking our bearings. If we have enjoyed much pleasure and peace, our serenity will show.

Some people look lively, fully present, or excited. Others look remarkably sad, deflated, or weary. All of us go through different moods and feelings, and our looks change accordingly throughout the day. But one look remains predominant. Let us note that look now and see if it suggests to us any place where change is needed in our inner landscape.

Looking in the mirror today, I read what my look tells me.

Death

The last Night that She
     lived
It was a Common Night
Except the Dying—this
     to Us
Made Nature different.

EMILY DICKINSON

When we come close to death through the death of our loved ones, life comes more alive for us even as we fill with sadness. Small aspects of nature come to our attention. We hear the song of birds more distinctly. We feel the rain or snow, as if it is falling to caress us.

By midlife many of us have lost one or both parents. Chances are we have also lost someone near our own age. These losses remove our youthful illusions of immortality and show us how life shimmers and then is gone, at least from these bodies. We receive this lesson by deepening our appreciation of the life we have now. From the deaths of others, we awaken more fully to these current moments of our lives.

I let death remind me of the transitory nature of my life, which is here to be enjoyed now.

Being Alone

I thought: "It's now or never. Either I cling to everything that's safe and that I know, or else I develop more initiative, do things on my own."
  And so it was that five days later I started for Baghdad.

AGATHA CHRISTIE

Some of us find ourselves unexpectedly alone in midlife. Or despite our family connections, we discover that we sometimes need to go off on our own in order to develop. This can feel like risky business. We may feel such adventures would better be left to the young; we are too old for exploring new territories.

But we might also use our age to realize we are experienced world travelers, even if we have only stayed at home, and this experience will benefit us if we choose to make the effort.

Taking the risk to go somewhere alone can ultimately be exhilarating. We each have places that call out to us. They may be as far away as a foreign country or as close as a walk in the nearby woods. When we respond to these calls, we receive the gift of discovery—new knowledge of ourselves.

Today, I will choose one place that draws me and go there on my own.

Fulfillment

My life has deepened unspeakably during the last year: I feel a greater capacity for moral and intellectual enjoyment, a more acute sense of my deficiencies in the past, a more solemn desire to be faithful to coming duties, than I remember at any former period of my life. . . . Few women, I fear, have had such reason as I have to think the long sad years of youth were worth living for the sake of middle age.

GEORGE ELIOT

How is it that youth gets the feature billing as the ideal time of life? Many people report the sense of feeling better with each passing year. Many of us survive a fairly precarious youth to grow into ourselves only at midlife.

George Eliot felt a "solemn desire to be faithful to coming duties." This is a sense of commitment to the fulfillment of self, a peace with one's purpose. No longer do we have to be feeling our way through prospects: Is this my direction or that? Many of us have found a path that offers harmony, at least in some aspect of our lives, and have discovered the satisfaction of following out this path. And many of us are relieved to have youth behind us.

Today, I take an honest look at the satisfactions of my life.

Destiny

We seek to "kiss the sky," because earth is our home, not our destiny. Our destiny is a better universe where we can live together in peace and under-standing.

NIKKI GIOVANNI

What a beautiful home we have been given. If we comprehend this—that the sky is our ceiling, the earth is our floor, the mountains are our walls, and the desert is our great room—then perhaps we can rise to our destiny, which takes our best effort.

Our world is still plagued by wars. Our streets are ravaged by poverty and the violence that grows out of desperation. People with few resources to satisfy their longings turn upon others of a different color, a different lifestyle, a different religion. Our destiny is to mature into a more peaceful society.

We who are in midlife now approximate this struggle in our one-on-one battle to accept and love ourselves as we are. Let us seek to open more resources to ourselves rather than turning upon others and to show by our example the way to a peaceful existence.

My destiny is joined with the destiny of the world
I live in. I take my part in it.

Ruts

The hardest thing to believe when you're young is that people will fight to stay in a rut, but not to get out of it.

ELLEN GLASGOW

In youth many of us felt as if we could not wait for the next change. Time moved too slowly for us. We wanted to graduate as soon as possible. We wanted to get out in the world and be on our path. We never dreamed that we might one day get in a rut and want to stay there and not have the "umph" to get out of it.

By midlife most of us have discovered our fondness for the old and familiar. We have realized the comfort of habits, even addictions, despite their ever-demanding drain on us. Often we spin around in the ruts of our obsessions and feel as if we are going nowhere. Only pain keeps us from being content with this status.

Menopause is a time for getting out of old ruts, for it is a time of reassessment. It is a time for us to focus anew. Even though we may encounter a long period of low energy, we are aware that we are brewing for a new emergence.

I use my menopause as a time to move out of old ruts.

Faith

Faith is found here, not in a destiny raiding and parceling out knowledge and the earth, but in a people who, person by person, believes itself. Do you accept your own gestures and symbols? Do you believe what you yourself say? When you act, do you believe what you are doing?

MURIEL RUKEYSER

Many of us are plagued by self-doubt. We hear ourselves saying something, then we wonder if we truly believe it. Or perhaps we adamantly believe what we are saying, but we take no actions to back up our belief. If we are afraid to make a firm commitment to that which we believe, we frustrate ourselves and feel incomplete.

Let us examine our beliefs now and have enough faith in them to stand behind them with our actions. For instance, if the experience of our aging is a rich one, let us believe in that and keep the faith even when we are barraged with messages that would contradict it. Let us act on our belief by continuing to expand our wisdom and take up our space by showing our wisdom to the world.

I have faith in myself today; the truth is present in my spirit.

Frustration

A measure of frustration
is an inevitable accom-
paniment to endeavor.

**ANNA LOUISE
STRONG**

We yearn for a smooth ride without
bumps or setbacks. Sometimes when we
encounter forces that thwart us, we turn
back, thinking we are on the wrong
road. Although there are times when it is appropriate for us to
turn back, we must take into account that, inevitably, when
we participate fully in life we encounter frustration. Doors do
not always open quickly or readily. Just as in fairy tales, the
hero often finds his or her direction and then must encounter
at least three trials, including temptations to be distracted or
thwarted from the journey, before he or she finds the way.

When we meet with frustration, let us appreciate that it
means we are making a life of endeavor. If we live an isolated
and withdrawn life, we may encounter little rejection or dis-
approval. However, we may be filled with the poisonous envy
of the unlived life. Better to respond to our desires and go for
what we want, expecting some forces to spar with us along
the way.

*I look at the up side of frustration; it means that
I am engaged.*

Paradox

We could never learn to be brave and patient, if there were only joy in the world.

HELEN KELLER

Life presents us with opposites, forcing us to learn to live with paradoxes. For instance, when we experience joy, we quickly feel the impulse to hang onto it forever. We want only the good stuff. We no longer want our lives to be fluid if it means that we will fall into a more difficult feeling state. But, alas, we deaden our joy when we try to hold onto it too tightly.

We learn to be brave and patient by encountering difficult feelings and problems. We are indebted to them for our deepening development. They show us our strength and our resourcefulness. They challenge us not to live on the surface of things but demand that we go below the surface.

Life matters more to us because we know that we will die. Joy springs forth a great lightness in our hearts at the end of deep sadness. Let us not try to hold it but to appreciate each moment of its presence.

I am grateful for the presence of each feeling that comes to me.

Confronting Transition

She had not expected [to be a middle-aged woman with grown children and not enough to do] this summer. Next summer, or the year after that, yes, but not *now*. What she had set herself to face had been all in the future. But it was *now* that it was happening.

DORIS LESSING

Many women begin to face their midlife transition when their children grow up and leave home. But even those of us who have no children are likely to be caught thinking that whatever it is we have to face is still in the future, when in fact it is not. Our midlife is a passage we gradually awaken to. The earlier we awaken the more consciously we will seek and find its rewards.

When we stick our heads in the sand and refuse to confront a transition that Nature requires of us, we only lose ground. For to deny Nature we must live in a place of fantasy, split from reality. If we try to grow younger in our minds while our bodies are growing older, we create separation within ourselves, when what our transition wants is integration. When we confront our transition willingly, new ground offers itself immediately and the pleasure of exploration is ours.

Today, I open myself to my midlife transition, its demands and its rewards.

Peace

> Peace is when time
> doesn't matter as it
> passes by.
>
> **MARIA SCHELL**

When we run from facing ourselves, it never seems as if there is enough time. It is as if time speeds up to keep one step ahead. We have no peace of mind. We function as if we are driven by unseen forces. Rest and relaxation become enemies rather than welcome friends. Many of us function through a good part of our youth this way, letting avoidance drive us in our careers and other ambitions but enjoying few moments of peace.

In midlife most of us come to put a higher premium on peace and serenity. We still have ambition, but we want to keep it in perspective with other values. We stop and face memories or problems that we have always run away from, and each time we do, we discover a new freedom—the pleasure of being at peace with ourselves.

In a state of peace time appears to slow down. We hear things we have blocked out before, such as the deep-throated glug of a bullfrog or the full music of an orchestra. We see the vibrancy of colors. We feel the essence of the universe all around us and within us.

I treasure peace more and more deeply as
I grow older.

Mothers

Kali allows us to understand that our personal mothers are not to blame for what is in the nature of human life. She links us to the blood and bones of our female knowledge, to our mothers' suffering as well as our own.

NAOMI RUTH LOWINSKY, PH.D.

In our youth we blame our mothers for much of our misery. We feel how they held us back and restricted us, suffocating us with love, or with the imposition of their unmet desires for themselves, or with neglect. Much of this is true, and we must examine it and rail against it and learn to give solace to ourselves where we are wounded. Kali, our dark Goddess, guides us as we descend into our darkness to do this work.

But by midlife many of us come out into a new dawn in which we settle these accounts with our mothers, forgive them, and become aware of the limitations of their humanity as well as those of our own. Now we can know their suffering without being concerned that it will obliterate ours. Now we can know more of human nature.

I can come out of the shadow of my mother into a new dawn.

Nature

What a world this is. Where else could water rise up to the sky, turn into snow crystals, magnificently brought together, fall from the sky all around us, pile up billions deep, and catch the small sparks of sunlight as they return again to water?

LINDA HOGAN

It is hard to remain depressed or self-absorbed when we take a clear-eyed look at Nature. She has so many aspects. She shows us how ever present change is. She shows us how inevitably the new season comes marching in and the old one fades out, regardless of our impulse to cling to one over the other.

Like the cycle of water transformed into snow, we also transmute and transform as we go through our process. Sometimes when we go through transitions, we feel as if we are falling apart. We feel lost and useless, and say, "What is the good of this?" But we continue to seek our direction in the dark. And mysteriously, both with our efforts and with some less tangible support from a higher source, we reach a place where we feel reconstituted.

Today, I let Nature guide me by her examples.

Ancestors

They touched earth and
   grain grew.
They were full of
   sturdiness and
   singing.
   My grandmothers
were strong.

MARGARET WALKER

We have a long lineage of ancestors behind us. Let us allow them to energize and guide us.

When our parents and grandparents pass over into the spirit world, they become freed from their earthly baggage. We still carry ours, and often we hold onto feelings about our parents and grandparents that keep us relating to their past offenses rather than to their now pure spirits. As we move through examining this baggage, we are able to receive the foundation they provided us.

Our grandmothers moved into their older ages with few comments. But we saw their wisdom, and we heard their songs. We honor them now by accepting our age with grace and pride.

I remember the beauty and strength of my grandmothers.

Trust

For things will surely
work out
by themselves.

CECIL BØDKER

Most of the time we compound a problem by trying to understand it too
quickly. When we step back we often
see a workable solution, or we see that
the problem needs more time to show us the solution. Our
perimenopausal and menopausal years are a good time to
consciously acquire more patience, giving things time to
work out for themselves. After all, this process parallels what
is going on in our bodies.

Of one thing we are quite sure—we cannot control the
changes that are taking place in our bodies. We may be able
to mediate and alter some of our responses, either with Hormone Replacement Therapy or with herbal remedies, yet
there is no doubt that our bodies are transforming. Some of
us have hot flashes on the hour. Some of us begin to lose hair.
Some of us wake in the middle of each night, flushed and
alert and unable to sleep. We are challenged to experience
these changes without struggling with them. We are challenged to release resistance and trust our bodies to the
process.

*I trust and let my body make this passage without
resistance.*

Freedom

What liberty a loosened
spirit brings.

EMILY DICKINSON

We seek liberty all through our lives.
First we are eager to grow up and have
the freedom of adults. Then we discover
how many of our constraints are within us. We try to fit
within the collective images of our family, our community,
our nation while searching for our individual self. We have an
urge to fit and belong as well as an urge to stretch and break
free.

There is a certain liberation in growing older. Restraints
that once seemed important to abide by fall away as we realize our time is limited and it is essential to allow ourselves to
be at ease. We care less about comparing ourselves to others
and more about being satisfied with ourselves.

It is in our spiritual connection that we find the greatest
liberty. For here we have a constant voice to guide us, whenever we are still enough to listen. Here we have an authority
that comes from within and requires no rebellion to give us a
sense of ourselves.

Guided by my spirit, I wear life like a loose garment.

Light

The soul can split the sky
in two,
And let the face of God
shine through.

**EDNA ST. VINCENT
MILLAY**

The spirit of Christmas is the spirit of renewal, symbolized in the birth of the Christ child. Whether or not we are Christians, we can let it be a joyful day in which our soul is attended through awareness. It is a day of giving and receiving, a day when we open our hearts to the music and the mysteries of life.

We can appreciate the deepening values we are growing into with midlife. The superficial glitz that might have once excited us does not satisfy as much as the simpler gifts we offer without expectation. A gift of gratitude to someone who has helped us throughout the year, a gift of service to help others less fortunate, such as the homeless, the gift of a phone call to let others know we love them and are thinking of them.

What is renewed is the light in each of us. Let us look for this light and see that it is the way in which we are all connected.

Today, I let my light shine through.

Pleasure

Most plans of life are too
strict. I allow a liberal
margin for pleasure.

VIRGINIA WOOLF

Especially as we come into our midlife years and realize we want our energy to plow the fields that will reap the greatest yield, we become aware of the merits of planning. Planning can be fruitful as long as it does not hem us in and is broad enough to embrace us fully.

Too often we plan only for work and not for play. Or we hold ourselves to an overly ambitious plan and castigate ourselves for the inability to complete it. If we look at our plans, do we see that they include pleasure? Do we allow ourselves to break them when new discoveries send us in a different direction?

If we have a tendency to put off pleasure, what better way to be sure we have some than to plan for it as we would plan for getting our work done?

Today, I will plan to receive a generous supply of pleasure.

Rebirthing

Loss of fertility does not mean loss of desire and fulfillment. But it does entail a change. . . . The woman who is willing to make that change must become pregnant with herself, at last. She must bear herself, her third self, her old age, with travail and alone.

URSULA K. LE GUIN

Do we look upon the opportunity to give birth to ourselves as exhilarating or are we daunted by it? Many of us have been through the labor of delivering our children and the protracted labor of raising them. Yet the idea of giving birth to ourselves may make us feel as if we are rock climbers hanging from a fingerhold on a cliff. For this is not a path well worn in our minds. Our society does not honor this passage. We did not hear our mothers laud their arrival at the outpost of older women.

We are fortunate enough to be aging at a time when menopause taboos are being broken. Women our age have been recording their experiences of this for over twenty years now. It is time we embrace this chance at a second birth for ourselves and consider our menopause a pregnancy, gestating all that we are still to become.

To give birth is to give the gift of life; I am pregnant with my older self.

Language

> Language exerts hidden power, like the moon on the tides.
>
> **RITA MAE BROWN**

The language that has been used to describe aging women is deeply inscribed in each of us. Phrases like "old bag," "over the hill," and "*little* old lady." Words like "shriveled," "hag," and "prune." As we enter menopause, we find ourselves repelled by our bodily changes when they conjure up these words. For instance, if we look in the mirror and, smiling, notice how our facial skin appears loose enough to be almost masklike, the phrase "old bag" pops into our head and makes us turn away from ourselves at exactly that moment when our changes desire a full embrace.

We hold the power to revise the language of aging. We cannot control how others use it, but we can begin to set an example by making our own usage caring and careful. We can take some of these words and turn them on their heads, as Mary Daly has done with "hag," charting how a hag is the most well developed of wise women, one who threatens those with less security into name calling. We can also create new images of aging women by using the power of language.

Today, I put my truth as an aging woman into the words that affirm me.

Self-satisfaction

I am proud of being
fifty-eight, and still alive
and kicking, in love,
more creative, balanced,
and potent than I have
ever been.

MAY SARTON

From looking through birthday cards about aging, we easily gain the impression that everyone would prefer to remain younger. When we tally the actual experience, we find many women who are very pleased to be the age they are.

Pleased to discover, as May Sarton did, new love, new potency, a surplus of creativity, and the ability to hold this full bouquet in a balanced harmony.

For many women menopause seems to be the time when creativity flowers fully. Perhaps some of our creative energies were earlier fulfilled by motherhood. Perhaps we have always been creative but were dampened by self-criticism or lack of self-confidence. With aging comes the benefit of accumulated experience, with which we build confidence. We also realize our days are passing by, never to be reclaimed, and we might as well care more for our opinion and less for that of others.

*I am pleased with myself for being exactly who I am
at my age today.*

Feelings

An astounding observation: it is precisely for feeling that one needs time, and not for thought. . . . Feeling is apparently more demanding than thought.

ANNA TSETSAEYVA

In the midst of a crisis, we feel little. We often seem to be recording the scenario for later playback, when we will have the luxury of slowing things down and allowing our feelings to emerge through the stimulus of our memory. If we are afraid of our feelings, perhaps we never do slow down. We stay "in our head" as much as possible. We may be great thinkers, but eventually we still yearn for the additional dimension of feeling.

As we grow older, we realize the value of our feelings, both painful and joyful ones. We realize how they texture life, which is otherwise mere existence. We experience deprivation when we are emotionally shut down and find ourselves without them. Let us give ourselves time on these occasions to go past thought to feeling. Let us not rush life so much we miss its texture and meaning.

I give feeling the time it takes to manifest fully.

Endings

We begin to see that the completion of an important project has every right to be dignified by a natural grieving process. Something that required the best of us has ended. We will miss it.

ANNE WILSON SCHAEF

Our midlife transition does not have a clearly defined ending like the ending of a year does. Even the declaration that we have finished with our menopause is rarely ever made. Yet the last day of the year may well be the one we use to reflect back and see what we have come through in recent times.

The ending of each project or process that we go through brings with it a little death, a grief that yearns for mourning. We often want to go right on through without taking the time to mourn, but let us be mindful that this is time well spent. For mourning allows us to leave the past behind and frees us for the present.

Perhaps the year's end is a good time for recording a few notes in a journal about where we are in our transition. Or perhaps we would enjoy bringing a few close friends together and sharing our year's harvest with them.

I honor the endings of my projects and transitions by acknowledging them.

The following are among the books I consulted and quoted from to compile this volume. I am indebted to these authors as well as to the authors of the many books not listed.

Barbach, Lonnie. *The Pause.* New York: Dutton, 1994.

Callahan, Joan C., ed. *Menopause, A Midlfe Passage.* Bloomington, IN: Indiana Univ. Press, 1993.

Cooper, Baba. *Over the Hill: Reflections on Ageism Between Women.* Freedom, CA: The Crossing Press, 1988.

Downing, Christine. *Journey Through Menopause: A Personal Rite of Passage.* New York: The Crossroad Publishing Co., 1989.

Friedan, Betty. *The Fountain of Age.* New York: Simon & Schuster, 1993.

Grahn, Judy. *Blood, Bread, and Roses.* Boston: Beacon Press, 1993.

Greer, Germaine. *The Change: Women, Aging, and the Menopause.* New York: Alfred A. Knopf, 1992.

Ojeda, Linda. *Menopause Without Medicine.* 2nd rev. ed. Alameda, CA: Hunter House, 1992.

Olsen, Tillie. *Silences.* New York: Delacorte Press/Seymour Lawrence, 1978.

Prétat, Jane R. *Coming to Age: The Croning Years and Late-Life Transformation.* Toronto, Ontario: Inner City Books, 1994.

Reitz, Rosetta. *Menopause: A Positive Approach*. New York: Viking Penguin, 1979.

Rountree, Cathleen. *On Women Turning Fifty*. San Francisco: HarperSanFrancisco, 1993.

Sand, Gayle. *Is It Hot in Here or Is It Me?* New York: HarperCollins, 1994.

Sang, Barbara, et al., eds. *Lesbians at Midlife: The Creative Transition*. Minneapolis, MN: Spinsters Ink, 1991.

Sarton, May. *Journal of a Solitude*. New York: W. W. Norton & Co., 1992.

Sheehy, Gail. *The Silent Passage: Menopause*. New York: Random House, 1992.

Sternberg, Janet. *The Writer on Her Work*. vol. 2, *New Essays in New Territory*. New York: W. W. Norton & Co., 1992.

von Franz, Marie-Louise. *The Feminine in Fairy Tales*. Boston: Shambhala, 1993.

Walker, Barbara G. *Women's Rituals: A Sourcebook*. San Francisco: HarperSanFrancisco, 1990.

Weed, Susun S. *Menopausal Years: The Wise Woman Way*. Woodstock, NY: Ash Tree Publishing, 1992.

Wilshire, Donna. *Virgin, Mother, Crone*. Rochester, VT: Inner Traditions, 1993.

Woodman, Marion. *Addiction to Perfection*. Toronto, Ontario: Inner City Books, 1982.

INDEX